# Molecular Gastronomy At Home

# Molecular
# Gastronomy
# At Home

## Taking culinary physics out of the lab and into your kitchen

JOZEF YOUSSEF

FIREFLY BOOKS

# A FIREFLY BOOK

Published by Firefly Books Ltd., 2013

Copyright © 2013 Quintet Publishing Ltd.

First Printing

**Publisher Cataloging-in-Publication Data (U.S)**
Youssef, Jozef.
    Molecular gastronomy at home : taking culinary physics out of the lab and into your kitchen / Jozef Youssef.
[256] p. : col. photos. ;   cm.
Includes index.
Summary: Molecular gastronomy techniques and recipes.
ISBN-13: 978-1-77085-201-3
1. Molecular gastronomy.  I. Title.
641.5 dc23    TX651.Y6877Mo   2013

**National Library of Canada Cataloguing in Publication Data**

Youssef, Jozef
    Molecular gastronomy at home : taking culinary physics out of the lab and into your kitchen / Jozef Youssef.
Includes index.
ISBN 978-1-77085-201-3
    1. Molecular gastronomy.  2. Cookbooks.  I. Title.
TX651.Y69 2013        641.5    C2013-901203-6

Published in the United States by
Firefly Books (U.S.) Inc.
P.O. Box 1338, Ellicott Station
Buffalo, New York 14205

Published in Canada by
Firefly Books Ltd.
50 Staples Avenue, Unit 1
Richmond Hill, Ontario L4B 0A7

Printed in China

This book was conceived, designed, and produced by
Quintet Publishing Limited
6 Blundell Street
London N7 9BH
Designers: Allen Boe,
Rod Teasdale and Michael Charles
Illustrator: Gareth Butterworth
Art Director: Michael Charles
Project Editor:  Margaret Swinson
Managing Editor: Emma Bastow
Publisher: Mark Searle

# CONTENTS

# FOREWORD BY CHARLES SPENCE

It is an incredibly exciting time for those of us who are lucky enough to be working at the cutting edge of gastronomical research and practice. On the one hand, cognitive neuroscientists are starting to uncover the rules by which the human brain combines information from each of the senses in the delivery of the flavors and textures of the food and drink that we all know and love (Spence & Piqueras-Fiszman, in press). The insights from this research, often referred to as "neurogastronomy" (Shepherd, 2012), or "gastrophysics," are now being utilized by many of the up-and-coming generation of young chefs who have been inspired by, and in many cases worked in the kitchens of, the pioneers of the modernist food movement such as Ferran Adrià in Spain and Heston Blumenthal in the UK. In fact, it was during his time working in the kitchens of The Fat Duck restaurant that I first met Jozef Youssef, a young chef whose passion was so very obviously to export the various tools and techniques of the modernist kitchen to various far-flung locations around the globe and to combine them with the amazing ingredients and techniques of these different regions.

It is certainly true that many of the modernist cooking techniques can be more than a little intimidating for the average home cook, not to mention requiring the purchase of some prohibitively expensive pieces of equipment (never mind, on occasion, some prohibitively expensive cookbooks: for example, see Blumenthal, 2008). As such, I am really pleased to see that, in this book, Jozef has taken up the challenge of making the insights of the modernist approach to cuisine accessible

to the masses. The various key techniques that he outlines in the following chapters require only the minimum of investment in terms of new equipment, or the purchase of unfamiliar ingredients. What's more, and for the first time that I have seen in print, the techniques are explained in a manner that any adventurous chef should be able to follow. Not only that, but as I am sure you will agree, the accompanying photography is both beautiful and inspiring. There are so many dishes here, and techniques that one wants to master in order to deliver what appear to be absolutely amazing spectacles of aesthetically pleasing visual design and intense flavor. Jozef's book will hopefully, in the coming years, come to stand proud alongside the likes of Harold McGee's classic 1990 book on the science of cooking, *The Curious Cook*, for any chef who really wants to master the science of what goes on in the kitchen.

For myself, as a psychologist interested in the human senses, there is nothing more multi-sensory than food and drink, stimulating as it does our sense of taste, smell, touch, vision, hearing and, on occasion, even pain — just think of the pleasant burn of chili or the sudden hit of wasabi at the bridge of the nose. Neglect any one of those sensory elements and the dish will be ruined. Ferran Adrià captured this notion perfectly when he said that, "Cooking is the most multisensual art. I try to stimulate all the senses." I am also really pleased to see that, toward the end of the book, Jozef guides the reader through the various senses and explains how they jointly contribute to the delivery of great-tasting foods. What you have then, dear reader, in the pages that follow, is both the art and the science of modernist cuisine laid bare in an accessible and easily digestible manner.

Research on the multi-sensory perception of flavor is throwing up some profound psychological and philosophical questions. My own research on flavor perception, conducted mostly in the lab, has benefitted enormously from my work with the likes of Jozef and other enthusiastic and talented young chefs, who have both the vision and creativity to take the best that neuroscience has to offer and turn it into something that is supremely satisfying on the palate — not to mention on the eye. These experimental chefs create novel culinary sensations that no diner has ever experienced before, or surprise the diner by making foods that look like one thing, but taste completely different. (If you need an example of this, just take a look at the mango spheres on page 46 — they look exactly like runny egg yokes.) Perhaps more importantly in the long term, the challenge for many of our biggest chefs, not to mention the food and flavor houses that often support their work, is to address the question of how to preserve the tastes and flavors of the foods we all know and love, while at the same time reducing the concentration of unhealthy ingredients such as salt, sugar and fat. I am a firm believer that the best of the insights derived in the kitchens of modernist chefs will, ultimately, hold the potential to improve the foods that we all eat on a daily basis. I am very hopeful, then, that the translational approach to modernist cuisine outlined here will impact positively on many of the multi-sensory experiences surrounding the consumption of food and drink that are, after all, among life's most pleasurable experiences. As Brillat-Savarin so aptly put it nearly two centuries ago, "The pleasures of the table belong to all times and all ages, to every country and to every day; they go hand in hand with all our other pleasures, outlast them, and remain to console us for their loss."

**Professor Charles Spence**

**Head of the Crossmodal Research Laboratory, Oxford University, UK**

# INTRODUCTION

So, you've decided to venture down the culinary avenue of molecular gastronomy! As with all cooking techniques, all that is required is some knowledge, tools and a lot of patience. "Molecular gastronomy" as a term does sound rather daunting, and some of the modern methods used on TV or in books can appear challenging if you've never tried them. However, once you begin reading this book and practicing some of the techniques, you will realize that modern cooking is as straightforward as any other form of cooking once you understand the underlying principles.

Before we go any further, it's important to understand what molecular gastronomy is about. By demystifying the term and giving ourselves a better idea of what the topic is and where it all started, we will gain a much better understanding of the culinary journey ahead. So let's go back to where it all began ...

The enjoyment of food starts long before taste — presentation is a key element of molecular gastronomy.

## A Brief History of Food Science

As far back as the ancient Greeks, food has been taken seriously as a science, with its medicinal properties being of great importance. This health-related view of food continues to be important today, and we have a thorough understanding of the nutritional content of the foods we eat and how they can impact our health. However, the food science that we are about to look at has more to do with the study of cooking techniques and our understanding of the physical and chemical reactions that take place in our food during the cooking process.

You may think that today's chefs are the first to bridge the gap between cooking and science, but discoveries in the 18th century were the first to have a real impact on how people cooked. The following are some of the milestones in the study of food science to show how far back this area of study goes.

**1700s:** One of the first names that stands out in the history of modern food science is that of French scientist Antoine-Laurent de Lavoisier, who is considered the father of modern chemistry. He constructed the metric system, named both oxygen and hydrogen, compiled the first extensive list of elements and studied the process of stock preparation by measuring its density to evaluate quality. When writing about his findings he noted, "whenever one considers the most familiar objects, the simplest things, it's impossible not to be surprised to see how our ideas are vague and uncertain, and how, as a consequence, it is important to fix them by experiments and facts."

The great chef Marie-Antoine Carême, who introduced a more elaborate style of cooking known as *grande cuisine* (the "high art" of French cooking) and served as a chef for French Emperor Napoleon Bonaparte, British King George IV while he was the Prince Regent, and the Czar of Russia, also took a scientific view when cooking. On the topic of stocks he said, "the broth must come to a boil very slowly, otherwise the albumin coagulates, hardens; the water, not having time to penetrate the meat, prevents the gelatinous part of the osmazome from detaching itself."

At around the same time Sir Benjamin Thompson, Count Rumford, an American-born physicist who studied the construction of fireplaces and kitchen utensils, worked to improve chefs' understanding of their work and kitchen tools; he also invented the double boiler, a kitchen range and a drip coffee pot.

Jean Anthelme Brillat-Savarin is still widely regarded as the father of modern chemistry. His famous aphorism "tell me what you eat and I will tell you what you are" has inspired chefs and nutritionists around the world.

**1800s:** In 1825 Jean Anthelme Brillat-Savarin's *The Physiology of Taste* was a culinary literary milestone, touching on both food science and philosophy. The book is a collection of anecdotes and essays on subjects ranging from chemistry, physiology and nutrition, to obesity, appetite, gourmandism, digestion, dreams, frying and even death. *The Physiology of Taste* is still in print today, and despite the fact that many of the ideas (particularly on food science) have now been proven wrong, its importance in food history remains prevalent.

It was also around this time that Justus von Liebig, an accomplished German chemist, developed a commercial production method for beef extract, the precursor to today's OXO stock cube. He was also responsible for one of the culinary world's greatest myths: that searing meat quickly at high temperatures seals in the juices (it doesn't!). The theory, published in 1847 in his book *Researches on the Chemistry of Food*, was disproven a long time ago, but many TV and celebrity chefs continue to propagate it.

At the turn of the 19th century, French scientist and food writer Édouard de Pomiane set out to debunk certain kitchen myths and demystify cooking by the use of science. He looked at the scientific principles behind several traditional techniques and explored the chemical processes that take place in his book *Cooking with Pomiane*.

**1900s:** During the latter part of the 20th century, Nicholas Kurti, a Hungarian-born physicist specializing in low-temperature physics, presented a television show in the UK called *The Physicist in the Kitchen*. The show, broadcast by the BBC in 1969, is considered a milestone in modern kitchen science since it brought the relationship between cooking and science into British living rooms for the first time. As part of the show Kurti amazed the audience by using the recently invented microwave oven to make a

reverse Baked Alaska — a frozen shell of meringue with a hot filling. At the time he explained, "I think it is a sad reflection on our civilization that while we can and do measure the temperature in the atmosphere of Venus we do not know what goes on inside our soufflés."

As an accomplished physicist and keen amateur cook, Kurti was key to the development of molecular gastronomy, and his work with French scientist Hervé This helped to establish and promote the study of the science of cooking.

Prior to this, food science research focused on areas such as food safety, microbiology, preservation, chemistry, engineering and physics. Much of it was carried out by big food manufacturers that wanted to improve the quality, look, taste and shelf-life of their products, or by biologists and scientists for whom cooking was a hobby. But cooking itself was never considered a serious field of scientific importance. Hervé This explained it as follows, "cooking was the last of the 'chemical arts' to become the object of scientific scrutiny and it still relies on telltale and anecdotal knowledge rather than solid science."

In 1984 the first real food science bible was published: Harold McGee's *On Food and Cooking: The Science and Lore of the Kitchen*. The scientific and historical culinary insights it contained were like nothing else published up to that point, and even for the next few decades, and the book remains a must-have for professional and amateur chefs alike.

### What is Molecular Gastronomy?

Initially, Nicholas Kurti called the field of study "science and gastronomy." However, when he and Hervé This were organizing the first workshop to bring together chefs and scientists, they were asked to come up with a more scientific title. Their solution was "molecular and physical

Frontispiece of *Le Patissier Royal Parisien*, a cookery book written in 1815 by Marie-Antoine Carême.

gastronomy," which was later shortened to "molecular gastronomy."

So, what is molecular gastronomy really about? It is a field of study that investigates the chemical and physical reactions and transformations which occur during the cooking process. It is important at this point to make one thing very clear: all cooking is science. There are scientific principles behind boiling water for a cup of tea or coffee, frying a steak, cooking pasta, boiling an egg, freezing ice cream and absolutely everything else you do in the kitchen.

Initially, Hervé This defined five main objectives for the field of molecular gastronomy in his doctoral dissertation. They were:

1. To collect and investigate old wives' tales about cooking.
2. To model and scrutinize existing recipes.
3. To introduce new tools, products and methods to cooking.
4. To invent new dishes using knowledge from the previous three aims.
5. To use the appeal of food to promote science.

However, This has since revised the objectives of molecular gastronomy as, "a particular branch of physical chemistry, looking at the mechanisms of phenomena occurring during culinary transformations." Regardless of the technical definition, foods created through the scientific techniques explained in this book are delicious, innovative and entertaining — whether they're labeled "molecular gastronomy," "molecular cooking," or "modernist cuisine."

### Popular Evolution of Molecular Gastronomy

In the mid-2000s the world's media introduced people to the term "molecular gastronomy" as a means of defining a new style of cooking that was beginning to emerge. A handful of restaurants were experimenting with this new approach and focused on the use of scientific principles to improve the quality, flavor and aesthetics of food. The approach became increasingly popular within culinary circles, and restaurants such as Ferran Adrià's El Bulli in Spain, Heston Blumenthal's The Fat Duck in England and Thomas Keller's The French Laundry in America received some of the world's top culinary accolades, being listed among the world's best restaurants and gaining three Michelin stars. The media started to use the term "molecular gastronomy," and further cemented its use for a style of food that was conceived using scientific principles and that focused on the best way to prepare the ingredients, which flavors work best together and how to present the dish.

Although it may have encouraged great publicity at the beginning, in time the term "molecular gastronomy" began to put many people off this new style of cooking, and it came to represent a concept that was too scientific, and not natural or organic, as many considered food should be. Some critics and chefs saw a reliance on science as being the opposite of what cooking should be about; they argued that cooking was an art and not a science. Many people became skeptical about the idea of "molecular gastronomy," coupled as it was with the use of strange and unfamiliar food additives, including liquid nitrogen, dry ice and gelling agents. The media's use of the term took it away from its original ideals, but many of the chefs who used scientific principles worked together to counter this. In 2006 Heston Blumenthal, Ferran Adrià, Thomas Keller and Harold McGee wrote a joint statement to inform people about their work and explain that they were merely using an understanding of existing scientific cooking principles to improve their food.

Famous chef, Ferran Adrià, preparing food at his restaurant, El Bulli.

Today the term "molecular gastronomy" has taken on a very broad definition that encompasses food created with a modern scientific approach, and even from a psychological and physiological perspective. In recent years, the world's top chefs have also devoted much time and effort toward looking at how we interpret food through all our senses, how we judge food based on our memories and associations and how all this impacts our perception of flavors: a field known as "multi-sensory flavor perception." Much research is also being done into the scientific methods of pairing flavors; this is referred to as "food pairing."

## About This Book

I hope that once you begin reading this book you will gain an even better understanding of what molecular gastronomy is about, that any misconceptions you have will be set straight, and that all your queries will be answered. It is important to remember that any type of cooking has scientific principles behind it, and that a good understanding of these principles will help you to improve your cooking.

As I've said before: all cooking is science. Hervé This has dedicated much time to the scientific phenomena that occur when an egg is "cooked" using different methods. His research has resulted in a number of discoveries, such as how to "un-cook" an egg, how to create up to 25 quarts (24 liters) of mayonnaise from a single egg yolk, the invention of a Béarnaise sauce made with chocolate instead of butter and the effects of cooking an egg at a low temperature (147.2°F/64°C) over a prolonged period of time (45 minutes).

This book aims to guide you through a number of the eye-catching or technically impressive techniques that have become associated with the more popular concept of molecular gastronomy. It will give you a good understanding of the science behind them, as well as the practical step-by-step guidance you need and some useful tips and tricks to try. Some of the techniques described (liquid nitrogen, the Anti-Griddle,

Many eye-catching techniques use basic kitchen methods with unusual ingredients like calcium lactate, a form of salt, pictured right.

centrifuge, rotary evaporator and ultra-sonic homogenizer) are impractical for the home chef; however they are at the cutting edge and are included in this book as they deserve attention.

I have also included chapters on topics such as food pairing, multi-sensory flavor perception and food presentation as they are topics that the world's leading chefs consider when they develop their menus. So if you have an interest in modern cooking, you're on the right track!

## A Note on Safety

The recipes and advice contained in this book do not represent a comprehensive guide to safety in molecular cooking. Always follow standard safety precautions when preparing food and adhere to instructions and guidance provided by equipment manufacturers. Some recipes containing meat, poultry and egg may not be suitable for small children or pregnant women.

This tender and flavorful oxtail with pommes purée and seasonal vegetables is easy to make if you have a water-bath and is sure to be a winner at any dinner party (see base recipe page 86).

## How to Use This Book

I recommend that you read each chapter from start to finish before attempting a technique, because understanding the science behind it, what you are doing and why will help you to achieve the results you want and will result in tastier food!

As this is not a regular cookbook, the recipes included act as a practical guide; don't allow them to constrain you or prevent you from inventing your own modern culinary creations.

Some techniques are more straightforward than others, and each requires different skills. I remember the first time I tried making Parmesan spaghetti using agar agar, I didn't get the right consistency until my fourth or fifth attempt, and as for reverse spherification, well that took me quite a few attempts to get the results I wanted! So my advice would be to persevere with the trickier techniques and keep practicing them until you get the required results.

It is also important to remember that, even though you are using modern scientific principles, the quality of the ingredients you use remains important: the better the ingredients you use the better your food will taste.

You will need some speciality tools and ingredients other than your normal kitchen equipment. Each chapter outlines the basic materials required; these tools, plus a few others.

Recipes are given in full, with ingredients and equipment lists, clear step-by-step instructions, and full-color photographs of the mouth-watering finished result.

## Equipment Icons

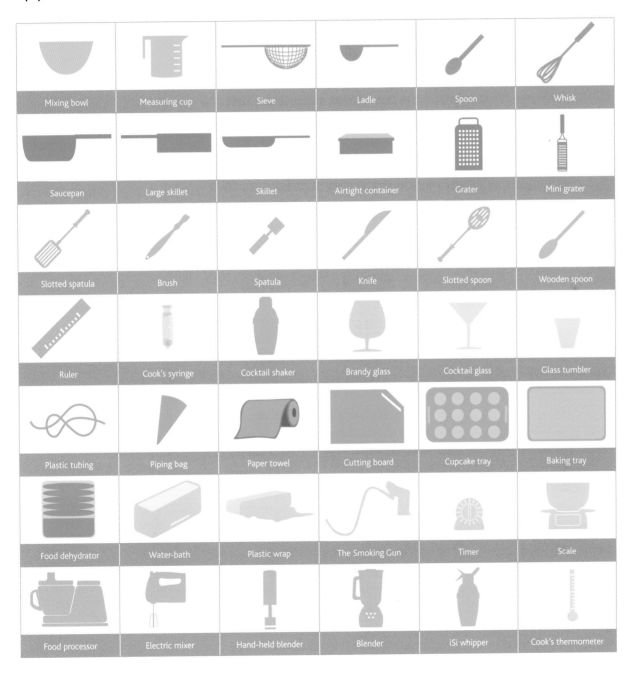

| | | | | | |
|---|---|---|---|---|---|
| Mixing bowl | Measuring cup | Sieve | Ladle | Spoon | Whisk |
| Saucepan | Large skillet | Skillet | Airtight container | Grater | Mini grater |
| Slotted spatula | Brush | Spatula | Knife | Slotted spoon | Wooden spoon |
| Ruler | Cook's syringe | Cocktail shaker | Brandy glass | Cocktail glass | Glass tumbler |
| Plastic tubing | Piping bag | Paper towel | Cutting board | Cupcake tray | Baking tray |
| Food dehydrator | Water-bath | Plastic wrap | The Smoking Gun | Timer | Scale |
| Food processor | Electric mixer | Hand-held blender | Blender | iSi whipper | Cook's thermometer |

# EQUIPMENT & MATERIALS

This book is all about teaching you techniques that are relatively new in the home kitchen and will add a certain flair to your dishes. But this means that there are a few pieces of equipment you will need before you get started. All the equipment suggestions listed below are readily available in speciality stores and online in most countries. In most cases they are very affordable purchases for those interested in taking their cooking to the next level. There are a few brands specifically mentioned as they stand out for their quality and durability and are used by professional chefs around the world. However, if you can find suitable substitutes that will get the job done, then go right ahead!

**Set of digital scales:** Ideally, the home cook needs two sets of digital scales. The first should measure in 1 g units — these types of scales will typically measure up to 5 kg and are good for calculating larger quantities and liquids. Many of these scales will also have a function that allows you to measure in milliliters, ounces and fluid ounces as well as grams. The second set of scales should measure in 0.1 g units — these scales are much more accurate and will help you to measure ingredients used in much smaller quantities, such as the powdered gelling and emulsifying agents employed in this book.

**Good-quality food blender/processor:** A good blender is invaluable to ensure that your purées are smooth and ingredients are thoroughly mixed. For this book I used a Thermomix, which should be every amateur and professional chef's dream kitchen gadget. Not only does it work as a blender, it also weighs, cooks, emulsifies, whips and steams ingredients. You can even cook a perfect risotto in it. It does of course come with a hefty price tag ($1,300), and a domestic brand of blender is perfectly fine.

A Thermomix food processor is a useful gadget for the kitchen because it performs many different functions.

When buying a blender, bear the following tips in mind:

- Always opt for a blender with several speed settings (the more the better).

- Choose a model that has a heat-resistant jug — polycarbonate and steel are less likely to crack than glass when hot ingredients are blended but have the disadvantage that you can't see what's going on in a steel jug, and polycarbonate can sometimes be flimsy.

- Manufacturers display a blender's power in watts. Most household models fall between 500 and 750 watts, but this information is not useful because it is a measure of the power consumed by the motor rather than the power generated by it — the force that causes rotation around a central point — to keep the motor from straining when it meets resistance. So to figure out what type of blender to buy, make sure you read lots of product reviews.

- Look for a blender with a removable blade as it will be much easier to clean!

If you want to spend a little more on a good quality blender then take a look at products by Vitamix (about $300), Blendtec (about $400) and Hamilton Beach ($15-50), all of which are good, powerful blenders and are slightly cheaper than the Thermomix.

**Hand-held immersion (or stick) blender:** These are must-have gadgets for any amateur chef, and a vital tool for a budding molecular gastronomist. They are basically an open-ended hand-blender that allows you to mix and blend ingredients in a bowl, and are ideal for mixing gelling agents into liquids and creating fantastic light foams and airs. Top end models start at $80 but many brands are affordable at $30.

**Water-bath:** This is a temperature-controlled water basin, which will cook foods at a particular heat for hours on end. They are extremely easy to use as all you have to do is fill the basin with water and set the temperature. For this book I used a water-bath manufactured by Clifton Food Range: it was accurate, durable and aesthetically pleasing. To date, most manufacturers produce water-baths for professional use and so they are not necessarily low in price ($300–$500). However, they are a useful piece of equipment for slow, temperature-controlled cooking, and make a fantastic addition to your range of kitchen appliances. Once you familiarize yourself with how a water-bath works, it will become an invaluable resource.

**Vacuum-packing machine:** These are advertised on many TV shopping channels and online, and can help you to store everything from food to clothes. Basically, they suck the air out of a bag or container, producing a vacuum, which reduces volume

Although some equipment can be expensive, many of the recipes (such as the yogurt spheres on page 44) rely on you having basic equipment such as measuring spoons and mixing bowls.

for storage and keeps the vacuum-packed items better protected from oxidization. Professional models come with an astronomically high price tag, so stick to a domestic model (most domestic models start at $100). The main drawback with domestic models is that you cannot vacuum-pack liquids in the plastic vacuum packing bags, but there are ways of getting around this that I explain in the chapter on sous vide (see pages 76–89).

**iSi whippers (espuma):** The professional chef's equivalent of a reusable whipped cream canister. You can use them with different liquids, gels and solids to produce a range of creams, foams and infusions. They can be used with both $N_2O$ and $CO_2$ gas cartridges and therefore can be used to make airy concoctions — or even fizzy ones! Best of all, they are reasonably priced ($50–$80) and should be a must-have for any chef. The iSi company produces a range of products, such as a funnel and strainer, which work with their product and make it even easier to use.

**The Smoking Gun:** A wonderful way to add a smoky flavor to your dishes without it being a hassle, messy or time-consuming. The Smoking Gun is produced by PolyScience, which is becoming a leader in innovative chef's tools and gadgets. This piece of equipment is reasonably priced (under $100) and easy to use. Once you have tested it out a couple of times the options will seem limitless.

**Food dehydrator:** This piece of equipment has the sole purpose of drying out foods at low temperatures over many hours. It's extremely simple to use — all you have to do is plug it in and set the temperature — and can be employed to dehydrate fruits, vegetables and meats, which all make great snacks. In this book I put it to use in a slightly more interesting way, but nonetheless all you need is a basic domestic food dehydrator to get started (domestic models start at about $30).

**Small molecular tools and other gadgets:** Syringes, PVC (Polyvinyl chloride) tubes and molecular slotted spoons are all useful when attempting some of the techniques in this book. Food tweezers, spherification spoons and silicone molds are not essential but will help with finishing touches. All of these gadgets can be bought online; for this book these useful (and pretty cool) utensils came from modernist-chef.com.

**Emulsifiers and gelling agents:** Many additives have gained a poor reputation over the years due to their use by industrial food manufacturers. However, I hope that this book (along with your own research into specific additives) will help to demystify them, showing that many of them have been in use for centuries by different cultures around the world, and that the majority are 100 percent natural. Emulsifiers and gelling agents are produced by many companies; the most popular ones that are readily available for home cooks include Sosa, Texturas, Kalys and Biozoon. It is important to bear in mind that even if they are the same gelling agent or emulsifier, the products by these manufacturers all have slightly different properties. This means the ratios and measurements required for a recipe may vary depending on which brand you use. In this book I have used Kalys and Texturas products, which are available from modernist-chef.com. So before using these additives, check both the product and manufacturer. Also, to get the best results when mixing additives, use ones from the same brand together as in general the final result will be better.

These beautiful eggless meringues are achieved using food dehydration equipment (see recipe page 141).

# TECHNIQUE 1: SPHERIFICATION

Spherification is a culinary process in which flavored liquids, such as alcohol, purées and juices, are manipulated using a gelling agent to form a thin membrane around the liquid. The process produces sphere-shaped capsules that burst in the mouth. The spheres are often referred to as "caviar," "ravioli" or "bubbles."

The thin membrane created in the spherification process is the result of a simple gelling reaction that takes place between sodium alginate and calcium lactate. There are two forms of spherification: basic spherification and reverse spherification. Both techniques follow the same principles; however, based on the calcium content, acidity and alcohol content of the liquid to be used, one method may be preferable to the other.

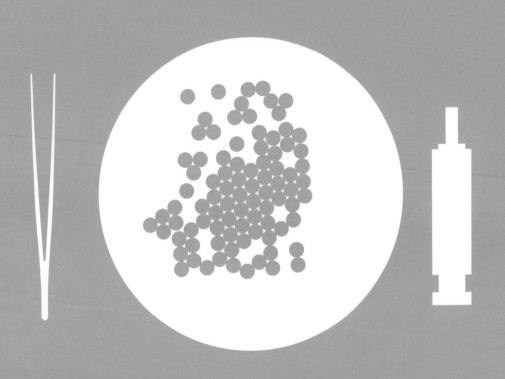

## Brief Background

The concept of spherification was originally developed by the pharmaceutical industry in the 1950s. The technique was refined and tweaked for use in professional kitchens around 2003, when chef Ferran Adrià of El Bulli restaurant in Spain introduced the culinary world to the process of basic spherification, and two years later his research team developed the reverse spherification process. Spherification has since become the quintessential molecular gastronomy technique and is as impressive now as when it was first developed.

The main gelling component involved in the spherification process is sodium alginate, which is extracted from brown algae. It has been used in the food manufacturing industry as an additive in soups, jellies, ice cream and sauces as a flavor enhancer, stabilizer and thickener, or both.

## The Science Behind the Technique

Spherification starts with dissolving sodium alginate and calcium lactate (sometime called calcium chloride) in two separate liquids (one flavored, the other water). Once the two are well dispersed in their respective liquids they are left to settle for a period to allow any trapped gases to be released, otherwise there will be air bubbles in the sphere. The next step is to take the flavored solution using a pipette or syringe — larger spheres are made using measuring spoons — and carefully squeeze drops of it into the water-based solution. The drops will instantaneously form a gel-coating once the two liquids come into contact. They are then left to "cook" in the water-based solution; the length of time will depend on the desired thickness of the sphere's membrane. Next the drops are removed and rinsed in a plain water-bath to remove excess calcium, which may inhibit the flavor. At this point the drops are ready to be served.

Mango Spheres is a classic example of basic spherification — pictured here with coconut rice pudding and passion fruit (see base recipe page 46).

## Basic Spherification

This is the simpler of the two forms of spherification. I definitely advise that you try this technique first as it will lay the foundations and basic understanding of how the process works and the expected outcome, which will help when you are approaching the slightly trickier reverse technique.

For this method the sodium alginate is dispersed into the flavored liquid (which will become the sphere) and the calcium lactate is dissolved in the water-bath (in which drops of the flavored sodium alginate solution will be "cooked").

Basic spherification is ideal for obtaining spheres with an ultra-thin membrane. The thinness of the membrane means there is more of the liquid inside the sphere and it requires less pressure to break through the surface, resulting in a better popping sensation in your mouth.

This method does have its limitations, however. The gelling process that takes place between the sodium alginate and calcium lactate is continuous. Therefore the "caviar" or "ravioli" will continue to gel until they become solid gel balls, so for full impact they must be served as soon as they are made. Another limitation is that the process will not work with liquids that have a high acidity (lower than pH 5) or calcium content. Although the liquid's acidity can be corrected using sodium citrate, this will affect the flavor.

When performing basic spherification, add liquid to the calcium bath one droplet at a time and the drops will "cook" for 5 minutes, forming spheres.

## Equipment and Ingredients

1.  Sodium alginate (E401)

    Extracted from brown seaweed, this is a "cold" gelling agent, so it does not require heat to gel. In the presence of calcium and acid it forms durable gels. Its most common use in the modern chef's kitchen is for the spherification process. Sodium alginate is available from modernist-chef.com.

2.  Calcium lactate (E327)

    A crystalline salt made by the action of lactic acid on calcium carbonate. It is commonly used as a form of calcium in food manufacturing and can be found in a wide range of edible products, from fresh fruits to infant foods. It is commonly used in the spherification process as, unlike other calcium products such as calcium chloride, it does not mask the flavor of foods or add any undesirable flavor. Calcium lactate is available from modernist-chef.com.

3.  Pipette or syringe (for "caviar")

    For the purpose of dropping well-shaped small spheres into either a calcium lactate or sodium alginate bath, an ordinary pipette or syringe is the best piece of equipment.

4.  Rounded measurement spoon

    To create really well-formed spheres with a nice, even, rounded finish, this type of spoon is very useful. You can use other tools; however, this will give you the best results.

5.  Slotted spherification spoon

    The name of this piece of equipment makes it sound a lot more technical than it really is. Basically it is a really small (and pretty cool-looking) slotted spoon that allows excess water to be drained from spheres or "caviar."

### Reverse Spherification

This is basically a reversal in terms of the liquids in which the sodium alginate and calcium lactate are dispersed. For this method the calcium lactate is dispersed into the flavored liquid (which will become the sphere) and the sodium alginate is dissolved in the water-bath (in which drops of the flavored calcium solution will be "cooked").

This process is far more versatile than basic spherification and can be used to form spheres with liquids that are high in dairy, alcohol or acidity. An even greater advantage is that spheres can be made in advance and served later, without compromising texture or flavor, as the gelling process stops once the spheres are removed from the sodium alginate bath and rinsed in water.

The spheres produced using this method will have a thicker membrane than those created using the basic technique. This is great for plating, as the spheres hold their shape better. However, it does give them a more solid and gelatinous texture in the mouth.

Forming nicely shaped spheres can be a little tricky as the sodium alginate solution is viscous. It is important that the calcium-based solution be thick enough to form spheres; if the liquid is too thin the spheres will be "deformed." The spheres must also be kept apart while in the sodium alginate bath as, if not, they will stick together.

Apple Caviar served in a caviar tin is an El Bulli restaurant classic (see recipe page 42).

## Tips

1. Be prepared for it to take up to 5 minutes for sodium alginate to disperse fully into water using a hand-held immersion blender.

2. Leave the sodium alginate solution to rest in order for the trapped air bubbles to escape. This can take up to 24 hours, especially with the sodium alginate bath used for reverse spherification, so prepare in advance and leave in the refrigerator.

3. For basic spherification, if the liquid in which the sodium alginate is to be dispersed is too thick — a purée, for example — mix the sodium alginate in water then add the flavored liquid; the sodium alginate should make up around 1 percent of the water and flavored liquid solution.

4. For basic spherification, mix the sodium alginate into one-third of the liquid, then add the rest of the liquid. This reduces the number of air bubbles that will become trapped in the solution.

5. For reverse spherification, allow the sodium alginate bath to come to room temperature before using it, to reduce the solution's viscosity.

6. For reverse spherification, pour the calcium-rich solution into the sodium alginate bath very carefully in order to achieve the right shape; this can take a lot of practice.

7. For reverse spherification, rotate the spheres while they are in the sodium alginate bath to ensure that the full surface area of each sphere is "cooked" equally and has a uniform membrane thickness on all sides.

8. Do not mix sodium alginate into tap water or mineral water if it has a high calcium content as this will trigger the gelling process before you have even started.

9. Keep the calcium (for basic spherification) or sodium alginate (for reverse spherification) bath clean; any small particles floating around from previous spheres that have ruptured may disturb the process. Simply use a fine sieve to remove any particles.

10. Make sure that spheres are fully immersed in the bathing solution by gently pushing them down or turning them.

11. For the recipes in this section the term "clean water-bath" refers to regular water in any receptacle and not the heated type of water-bath equipment mentioned in other chapters.

Strawberry and Balsamic Spheres require the Basic Spherification technique (see base recipe page 42).

# APPLE "CAVIAR" (BASIC SPHERIFICATION)

### INGREDIENTS
1 tsp (5 g) sodium alginate
2 cups (500 ml) apple juice
1 tsp (5 g) calcium lactate
4 cups (1 L) water

**Serves 5**

1. Using your hand-held immersion blender, mix the sodium alginate into one-third of the apple juice. It may take a while to ensure the sodium alginate is well hydrated.

2. Add the remaining apple juice to the mixture and allow to rest in the refrigerator for at least 4 hours. This removes the air bubbles trapped during the hydration process in step 1 and gives the "caviar" spheres a smoother look.

3. While the apple mixture is resting, prepare the calcium bath by whisking the calcium lactate into the water in a large mixing bowl, making sure it is fully dissolved.

4. Fill a syringe (or pipette) with the apple mixture.

5. Place the tip of the syringe (or pipette) about 4 inches (10 cm) above the surface of the calcium bath; adjust the height to obtain the best-shaped spheres.

6. Gently squeeze drops of the apple mixture into the calcium bath and leave the "caviar" to "cook" for 1 minute.

7. Gently remove the "caviar" from the bath using a slotted spoon and transfer it to a clean water bath to rinse off any excess calcium on its surface. Remove and serve immediately.

### Serving suggestions

- Apple "caviar" served in a caviar tin (an El Bulli restaurant classic)

- Ginger cheesecake topped with apple "caviar"

- Mature cheddar and apple "caviar" canapés

- Apple "caviar" with fresh apple ribbons and tarragon (pictured opposite)

# YOGURT SPHERES (REVERSE SPHERIFICATION)

## INGREDIENTS

1 tsp (5 g) sodium alginate

4 cups (1 L) water

1 cup (250 ml) plain Greek yogurt (do not use low-fat yogurt as the calcium content is lower; if you do use a low calcium content yogurt, add ½ tsp/2.5 g calcium lactate)

4½ tbsp (70 ml) whole milk

**Serves 5**

1. Using your hand-held immersion blender, mix the sodium alginate into the water in a large mixing bowl. It may take a while to ensure the sodium alginate is well hydrated.

2. Allow the sodium alginate bath to rest in the refrigerator, ideally overnight, until all the trapped air bubbles have been released.

3. Whisk the yogurt and milk together to create a smooth mixture, but do not aerate it. If you are adding calcium lactate, this is the time to do so.

4. Using a rounded measurement spoon, scoop up the yogurt, making sure the sides of the spoon are clean (this helps to get a better shape).

5. Gently pour the yogurt into the alginate bath — this step takes lots of patience as getting the right spherical shape can be difficult, so practice, and remember it's all in the wrist action.

6. Allow the spheres to "cook" in the sodium alginate bath for 2–3 minutes, remembering to flip the spheres or gently push them down about halfway through the "cooking" time to ensure that they cook equally on all sides and that the membrane that forms has the same thickness all the way around the sphere.

7. Gently remove the spheres from the sodium alginate bath using your slotted spoon and place into a clean water bath. The spheres are now ready to be served, so you can serve them right away or store them in the water and refrigerate until you are ready to use them.

### Serving suggestions

- Yogurt sphere canapés with a drizzle of honey and sprinkle of hazelnut

- Deconstructed Indian raita: cucumber, red onion and a yogurt sphere dusted with cumin and cayenne pepper and topped with a baby mint leaf (pictured opposite)

- Fruit salad topped with yogurt spheres

# MANGO SPHERES (BASIC SPHERIFICATION)

## INGREDIENTS

1 tsp (5 g) calcium lactate

2 cups (500 ml) water

½ tsp (2.5 g) sodium
alginate

1 cup (250 ml) mango juice
(or other non-calcium/
non-acidic purée)

**Serves 3**

1. Prepare the calcium bath by whisking the calcium lactate into the water in a large mixing bowl and set aside once fully dissolved.

2. Using your hand-held immersion blender, mix the sodium alginate into one-half of the mango juice. It may take a while to ensure the sodium alginate is well hydrated.

3. Add the remaining mango juice to the mixture and incorporate using a whisk.

4. Using a teaspoon, scoop up the mango mixture and gently pour the mixture into the calcium bath and leave the bubble to "cook" for 1 minute in the bath, turning the bubble over halfway through the "cooking" time.

5. Gently remove the "sphere" from the bath using a slotted spoon and transfer it to a clean water-bath to rinse off any excess calcium on its surface. Remove and serve immediately.

### Serving suggestions

- Mango spheres served on a Japanese spoon

- Mango spheres on a bed of lime zest with hazelnut (pictured opposite)

- Mango spheres with coconut rice pudding and passion fruit

# TECHNIQUE 2: CULINARY SMOKING

In the present culinary wonderland there are a number of ways to impart a smoky flavor to your foods, but for the purpose of this chapter we will focus on liquid smoke and The Smoking Gun. Both techniques are very simple yet can add a fantastic additional layer of flavor to the right type of dish, or intensify an ingredient's existing smoky flavor. Note that "smokiness" is a flavor and will not necessarily affect the actual taste or texture of the food. So, for example, smoked mashed potato won't taste smoky if you pinch your nose while eating it.

Liquid smoke is produced by burning woodchips (of which there are many varieties: hickory, maple, apple, whiskey oak and so on) in a combustion chamber that fills with smoke. The smoke passes through a tube into a condenser where it cools and forms liquids or solids, which are then dissolved in water. The result is a dark-colored, bitter-tasting liquid with a pungent smoky aroma.

The Smoking Gun is a simple tool that allows foods to be infused with a smoky flavor, which would otherwise be very tricky, laborious and time-consuming using traditional methods.

## Brief Background

Smoking was initially used as a method of preserving and extending the life of food. Nowadays we have the resources — refrigerators and freezers, in addition to the preservatives in processed foods — to store our foods for longer periods than formerly without them spoiling. The purpose of the new methods of imparting a smoky flavor are really just for the flavor itself, as this can add a whole new dimension to a dish.

Liquid smoke was first bottled and sold in 1895 by Ernest H. Wright, an American pharmacy owner who experimented with the combustion of wood and the condensation of the resulting smoke into a liquid, which he termed "condensed smoke." Liquid smoke proved to be a suitable substitute for traditional smoking methods as far as flavor was concerned, and it has since been used by both industrial food manufacturers and home cooks alike.

The Smoking Gun, on the other hand, is a much more recent innovation. This revolutionary product was developed by an American-based company called PolyScience in their quest to produce more innovative tools for chefs. It is now widely used in restaurant kitchens all over the world.

## The Science Behind the Technique

Traditional smoking techniques impart a particular flavor to foods as a result of the chemical reactions that take place when wood is combusted. The main components of hardwood are cellulose, hemicellulose and lignin and it is these three elements that produce a smoky flavor. The flavor of the smoke depends on the ratios of these three components, which in turn is dependent on the species of tree.

Liquid smoke is a useful substitute for traditional smoking as it imparts an equally smoky flavor without all the fuss and labor involved in traditional methods. Adding a few simple drops of liquid smoke to a marinade, dressing, cooking liquid, cocktail or prepared food can add a whole new dimension to a dish.

Smoked Chocolate Sorbet with sour cherry sauce (see base recipe page 60).

## Infusing With Smoke

The Smoking Gun is a great way to infuse smoky flavors of varying degrees into almost any food or drink. The smoke produced is not hot and therefore it can be used to smoke ingredients such as butter or raw seafood (think smoked salmon sashimi), which would otherwise be very difficult and potentially hazardous (for reasons of food safety and temperature). The Smoking Gun can produce a great sensory effect when a completed dish is covered with a dome lid into which smoke has been added, allowing the diner to get a puff of delicious smokiness when they lift the cover.

## Preparation

The phenolic components that make the food "smoky" are volatile and will dissipate over time. So it is advisable, when using The Smoking Gun, to leave the smoking until you wish to serve the food. Much of this depends on the degree to which you smoke the food and the intensity of smokiness you want present in the dish.

## Tips

1. Liquid smoke does not have the most appetizing of flavors and is very powerful, so use it sparingly; a few drops usually does the job.

2. Liquid smoke is best mixed into liquids such as marinades or sauces, or soft foods such as mashed potato, so that it can disperse uniformly through the food. A couple of drops on a steak could result in some parts tasting more intensely of smoke than others.

3. Experiment with smoking different foods, such as shellfish, red meats, poultry, cheese, butter, chocolate and so on.

4. Most fats and oils will absorb odors and flavors quite readily, so by smoking butter, for example, you then add a hint of smoky flavor to any dish you add the butter to.

5. Read and follow the instructions provided with The Smoking Gun. Once you have mastered the basics of how it works, the world is your oyster ... which you may even consider smoking.

The Smoking Gun makes an excellent smoky rum cocktail. See recipe on page 56.

### Equipment and Ingredients

1.  Liquid smoke

    This can be made in two ways: either by passing water through a chamber filled with smoke or by smoke being passed through a tube into a condenser with the resulting solids or liquids then dissolved into water.

2.  The Smoking Gun

    A wonderful way of adding a smoky flavor to your dishes without it being a hassle, messy or time-consuming. The Smoking Gun is produced by PolyScience, who are becoming leaders in innovative chefs' tools and must-have gadgets. The Smoking Gun is reasonably priced and easy to use. Once you have tested it out a couple of times, the options will seem limitless. An important point to note is that you are not confined to smoking just woodchips in The Smoking Gun; interesting culinary creations can be made by smoking teas, spices or even dried flowers.

3.  Woodchips

    These are used with The Smoking Gun and come in a variety of flavors, including hickory, applewood, mesquite and cherry. The type of woodchips you use will depend on the type of smoky notes that you want to match up with your dish.

4.  Cocktail shaker

    If you are going to make a cocktail then a shaker has got to be part of the process, as it allows for an even distribution of liquids and flavors.

# SMOKY RUM COCKTAIL

### INGREDIENTS

⅕ cup (50 ml)
  Captain Morgan
  original spiced rum
⅕ cup (50 ml) Kahlúa
  coffee liqueur
ice cubes
a dash of bitters
smoking chips

**Serves 1**

1. Take a clean old-fashioned or rocks glass and invert it over the tip of the Smoking Gun nozzle.

2. Fill the glass with dense smoke then immediately place the glass on a surface to trap the smoke and leave for 5 minutes without disturbing.

3. While the glass is sitting with the smoke inside it, pour the rum, Kahlúa and bitters into a cocktail shaker half-filled with ice and shake well.

4. Lift the glass to release the smoke, add a couple of ice cubes and immediately strain the cocktail into the glass.

## Alternative suggestions

·   Smoky Manhattan

·   Smoky Old-Fashioned

·   Smoky Moscow Mule

# COARSE SMOKED MUSHROOM PURÉE

## INGREDIENTS

olive oil

2 oz (57 g) shallots, diced

1 tsp (5 ml) garlic paste

13 oz (400 g) button
mushrooms, chopped

7 oz (200 g) portobello
or shiitake mushrooms,
chopped

1 oz (28 g) butter (optional)

⅔ cup (150 ml)
heavy cream

salt

smoking chips

**Serves 2**

1. Heat a little olive oil in a skillet and sweat the shallots until translucent, then add the garlic paste.

2. Add the mushrooms to the skillet and cook until they are golden in color.

3. Add the butter, if using, followed by the cream, and once the mixture has come to a boil, remove it from the heat and add salt to taste.

4. Transfer the contents of the skillet (while still hot) into a food processor and pulse until you have a coarse mixture (alternatively use a hand-held blender and mixing bowl as shown right).

5. Cover the bowl of the food processor with plastic wrap and use The Smoking Gun to fill it with dense smoke. Leave to rest for 5 minutes.

6. Remove the plastic wrap from the food processor and pulse again to incorporate the smoke further. For a stronger smoky flavor, repeat steps 5 and 6.

## Serving suggestions

- Smoked mushroom porridge with Parmesan air

- Grilled steak with smoked mushroom purée and beef jus

- Roast chicken breast stuffed with smoked mushroom, wrapped in bacon (pictured opposite)

# SMOKED CHOCOLATE SORBET

**INGREDIENTS**

1.9 cups (450 ml) water

6½ oz (190 g) granulated
sugar

1½ oz (40 g) brown sugar

3½ oz (100 g) unsweetened
cocoa powder

1 tsp (5 ml) vanilla extract

liquid smoke, to taste

**Serves 2**

1. Place the water and sugars in a saucepan and heat, stirring, until the sugar dissolves.

2. Whisk in the cocoa and bring the mixture to a simmer.

3. Remove the mixture from the heat and transfer it to a mixing bowl, then stir in the vanilla extract and liquid smoke. Place the mixture in the refrigerator for 2 hours.

4. Pour the mixture into your ice cream maker and follow the manufacturer's guidelines.

5. Once the sorbet is ready to serve, place each portion in a glass covered with plastic wrap and use The Smoking Gun to fill the glass with smoke. Leave to rest for 1 minute then allow your guests to remove the plastic wrap at the table — this adds a little more smoky flavor and a lot more showmanship to your dessert.

## Serving suggestions

- Smoked dark chocolate sorbet with sour cherry sauce (pictured opposite)

- Smoked dark chocolate sorbet and coffee ice cream

- Smoked dark chocolate sorbet with mint chocolate chips

# TECHNIQUE 3: AIRS, FOAMS & ESPUMAS

A culinary foam is a liquid, such as juice, purée, stock or soup, mixed with a gelling or stabilizing agent, such as lecithin, agar agar, gelatin or xanthan gum, which is then aerated using either a hand-held immersion blender or extruded through a reusable cream whipper using gas (nitrous oxide) cartridges. Foams are a great way to add an additional flavor element to a dish; they are also visually appealing.

There is no real difference between an air, a foam and an espuma other than the density of the resulting foam. An air is typically very light, foams are slightly denser, and an espuma is generally closer to the consistency of whipped cream. However, this is not set in stone and different combinations of tools and stabilizers will produce different outcomes.

## Brief Background

Despite its recent rise in popularity, this technique is not new. Foams have been around for a long time — meringues, mousses, marshmallows, cappuccinos and whipped cream are all types of foam — but it was chef Ferran Adrià of El Bulli restaurant in Spain who really developed the potential of foams by using the science behind them to produce the culinary foams, airs and espumas that are now used in kitchens all over the world. In fact, when Adrià developed this technique in the 1990s and shared it with the public, it took the culinary world by storm and began to appear on any menu wishing to appear avant-garde, regardless of whether the technique actually worked with the dish or added value in any way. Despite this, it is still a popular culinary technique that chefs have now begun to use more discerningly.

## The Science Behind the Technique

Put simply, foams are a dispersion of gas in a liquid; the more gas trapped in the liquid, the greater the volume of the foam. Almost all liquids will form bubbles when they are aerated. However, in many cases the bubbles will simply coalesce and burst quite rapidly. The trick with making a good foam is to get it to hold its form, which is achieved by introducing a surfactant (a compound that lowers the surface tension of a liquid) into the liquid to coat the surface of air bubbles, creating a thin barrier between the bubbles to prevent them coalescing.

It is important to note that culinary foams can be made without any added stabilizers: milk fat, cheese fat or even foie gras fat will form relatively stable foams. However, these foams will be much looser and will break down quicker than those made using added stabilizers, so they are best suited to serving as a light sauce or froth on a dish.

There are a number of stabilizers available to chefs nowadays that act as surfactants; this chapter will focus on lecithin, agar agar and gelatin.

A lecithin-based foam (see page 69) provides additional flavor and texture to asparagus and prosciutto with poached quail egg.

## Equipment and Ingredients

1. Hand-held immersion blender

   This is also known as a stick blender. It is a must-have gadget for any budding molecular gastronomist. It is basically an open-ended hand-blender that allows you to mix and blend ingredients in a bowl. They are great for mixing gelling agents into liquids and creating fantastic light foams and airs.

2. iSi whipper

   Sometimes called an espuma, this is the professional chef's equivalent of a reusable whipped cream canister. You can use it over and over with different liquids, gels and solids.

3. $N_2O$ and $CO_2$ gas cartridges

   Can be used to make airy or fizzy concoctions. Use carbon dioxide gas chargers for carbonation and nitrous oxide for foams.

4. Lecithin

   Most commercial lecithin is extracted from soybeans, making it vegetarian- and vegan-friendly. It is a very adaptable surfactant that will work on both acids and bases. It is commonly used with juices and other substances with a high water content. Lecithin is effective in creating foams — which are air/water emulsions — and in emulsifying water/oil mixtures, such as vinaigrettes and dressings.

5. Gelatin

   Gelatin is derived from collagen obtained from various animal by-products and is a very efficient foam stabilizer.

## Preparation and Cooking Times

**Fat-Based Foams:** All that is required for a fat-based foam is an appropriate source of fat in the recipe, such as milk, cheese, butter or foie gras, or meats like bacon or chorizo. These foams will need to reach a temperature of between 140°F (60°C) and 176°F (80°C) in order to hold a stable foam. Fat-based foams are produced using a hand-held immersion blender.

**Lecithin-Based Foams**: A concentration of around 0.5 percent to 1 percent of lecithin is enough to create a stable foam. Lecithin produces very good cold foams and is soluble in cold solutions. Its effectiveness is impaired at high temperatures, so anything up to 158°F (70°C) should produce a stable, high-yielding foam. Juices produce particularly good foams and are remarkably simple; all that is required is strained juice (such as carrot juice), to which 1 percent of lecithin is added and then blended/aerated with a hand-held immersion blender. Lecithin foams can be produced using either an iSi whipper or a hand-held immersion blender.

**Agar-Based Foams:** A concentration of around 1 percent of agar is enough to create a stable foam. Given its high temperature threshold, agar is very effective at producing warm foams. It is most soluble in solutions above 176°F (80°C), has a setting temperature of around 95°F (35°C) to 113°F (45°C) and when gelled, it has a melting point of around 185°F (85°C). Once the agar has been dispersed into the liquid and left to set the resulting gel should be warmed up to 158°F (70°C) and blended into a smooth, fluid gel consistency using a hand-held immersion blender. Once this has been achieved the gel should be poured into an iSi whipper, charged with nitrous oxide and kept at a temperature around 158°F (70°C).

**Gelatin-Based Foams**: A concentration of around 0.5 percent to 1.5 percent of gelatin is enough to create a stable foam. Gelatin is soluble in liquids at temperatures around 122°F (50°C) and sets at around 59°F (15°C). Before using a gelatin sheet it must be "bloomed" in water; once this has been done, it is ready to be dissolved into a warm liquid, then the mixture should be poured into an iSi whipper, charged with a gas cartridge and placed in the refrigerator to rest for at least 2 hours.

## Tips

1. iSi whippers must be shaken vigorously before every use.

2. Do not completely fill an iSi whipper.

3. Some iSi whippers are not intended to be used for hot preparations, so check the instructions.

4. Carbon dioxide gas chargers are also available for iSi whippers, although they are more suited to carbonation. For foams, stick with nitrous oxide chargers.

5. The viscosity of a liquid will impact on how the foam turns out. If a liquid is too thick and heavy, aerating it sufficiently to produce a foam may not be possible.

6. Strain liquids through a very fine sieve first.

7. Use a hand-held immersion blender to disperse lecithin and a whisk for agar or gelatin.

8. Adding too much lecithin will destabilize a foam.

9. If using gelatin sheets, "bloom" in ice water, squeeze out the excess water and dissolve in the desired liquid.

10. Ensuring the agar is well dispersed into a liquid which is 176°F (80°C) or higher is a very important step. The agar must be well hydrated in order to gel effectively.

# CHILLED STRAWBERRY FOAM

## INGREDIENTS

1⅕ cups (300 ml)
   strawberry purée
   (other fruit purées
   can be substituted)
⅖ cup (100 ml) water
superfine sugar, to taste
   (this depends on the
   sweetness of the purée)
1 leaf of gelatin or ½ tsp
   (2.5 g) gelatin powder

**Serves 5**

1. Pass the purée through a very fine sieve to ensure that it is very smooth.

2. Combine the strained purée, water and sugar in a saucepan and heat gently until the sugar has dissolved.

3. If using gelatin leaf, "bloom" it by soaking it in a bowl of cold water until it is soft, then remove it and squeeze out any excess water.

4. Whisk the gelatin into the warm purée, making sure it is well dispersed.

5. Pour the mixture into your iSi whipper, making sure not to fill it more than halfway.

6. Seal the top of the iSi whipper and charge with 2 nitrous oxide cartridges. Shake well and refrigerate for 2 hours.

## Serving suggestions

- Vanilla ice cream with strawberry foam

- Strawberry foam-topped cheesecake canapés

- Champagne flutes topped with strawberry foam (pictured opposite)

# CHORIZO FOAM

**INGREDIENTS**

8 oz (227 g) finely diced
    chorizo
1⅕ cups (300 ml)
    heavy cream
1⅔ cups (400 ml)
    whole milk

**Serves 5**

1. Place the chorizo in a cold, dry skillet over a low heat and allow the skillet to gradually heat up. As it does so, the dark red flavorsome oil in the chorizo will slowly begin to seep out into the skillet.

2. Once the chorizo has released most of its fat, add the cream and bring to a boil, then reduce the heat and simmer for 5 minutes.

3. Add the milk, bring to a boil once again, then remove the mixture from the heat.

4. Strain the mixture through muslin (cheesecloth), reserving the oil-rich chorizo cream and discarding the solids.

5. Allow the mixture to cool to around 158°F (70°C).

6. Use your hand-held immersion blender to foam the chorizo cream, incorporating as much air into it as possible. If the cream looks too thick, adjust its consistency by adding a little more milk.

## Serving suggestions

- Shellfish bisque with chorizo foam (pictured opposite)

- Squid ink risotto with pan-fried squid and chorizo foam

- Saffron rice with grilled chicken breast, king prawns and chorizo foam

# PARMESAN FOAM

## INGREDIENTS

2 cups (500 ml) water

1 lb (454 g) Parmesan cheese, freshly grated

¾ tsp (3 ml) lecithin

**Serves 5**

1. Bring the water to a boil in a saucepan, then remove from the heat and add the grated Parmesan, leaving it to infuse for 20 minutes at room temperature.

2. Strain the mixture through muslin (cheesecloth), reserving the "Parmesan water" and discarding the mushy Parmesan solids; they should be flavorless anyway as all the flavors have infused into the water.

3. Using a hand-held immersion blender disperse the lecithin into the "Parmesan water."

4. Continue using the hand-held immersion blender to aerate and begin to create a foam on the surface of the liquid.

5. Gently remove the foam using a spoon, repeating the aeration/foaming process (step 4) as many times as necessary, and fill an airtight container with the foam. Place the container in the freezer for 1 hour — you now have frozen Parmesan air.

## Serving suggestions

- Caesar salad with frozen Parmesan air (pictured opposite)

- Smoked mushroom porridge with Parmesan air

- Seafood pasta with Parmesan air

# TECHNIQUE 4: SOUS-VIDE COOKING

If you've never heard the term "sous vide" before, don't panic. As with many of the techniques in this book that may not be familiar to you at first glance, it is really quite simple once you break it down and gain an understanding of the basic principles. Sous vide literally translates to "under vacuum," and refers to the process of poaching food that has been sealed in an airtight, temperature-resistant plastic bag (vacuum packed) in a temperature-controlled water-bath. This typically involves cooking food at lower temperatures and for longer than when using conventional cooking methods. It's basically a very advanced cross between "boil in the bag" and slow-cooking techniques, but using more advanced tools to achieve consistent and uniform results.

Of all the techniques in this book, this is the most useful for everyday employment. It will improve aspects of your cooking and save you time, as foods can be slow-cooked in advance, refrigerated, then heated up to serve. In addition, vacuum-packed food lasts longer in a refrigerator, and unlike with some other cooking techniques, once you have prepared the food, vacuum-packed it and placed it in a water-bath, you can pretty much leave it unsupervised until its cooking time is up.

## Brief Background

This technique was discovered by American and French engineers in the 1960s, based on earlier research conducted by Sir Benjamin Thompson in the late 18th century. Its use in restaurant kitchens began in the 1970s with French chef George Pralus at the Restaurant Troisgros, and was further popularized by American chef Thomas Keller in 2008 in his book *Under Pressure: Cooking Sous Vide*. It is now commonly used in restaurants of all types — not just those considered modernist. What's even better is that the equipment used (which was once designed only for science laboratories and came with a high price tag) is now being produced for domestic use at more reasonable prices. Sous-vide cooking is expected to become a more popular technique for home cooks, so get started.

## The Science Behind the Technique

Chef George Pralus discovered that when cooking foie gras using sous vide he managed to retain its appearance, achieve a more uniform texture and lose less fat than when using conventional cooking methods. But this only begins to outline the actual benefits that lie behind this revolutionary method of cooking. In order to fully understand and use sous-vide cooking, it helps to have a basic idea of the science involved.

The sous-vide method stabilizes the temperature element in the "temperature–time" equation, as the water-bath in which the food is immersed is fixed at a set temperature (which is set before the food is put in the water-bath). This means that the entire surface area of the vacuum-packed food is surrounded by a uniform temperature with no variation for the duration of its time in the water-bath. This results in food that is evenly cooked all the way through, as opposed to results achieved using conventional cooking methods, which cook the outside of the food more than the inside.

The temperatures used are typically low and range from around 131°F (55°C) to 140°F (60°C) for meats and higher for vegetables. The advantage of such a low temperature when cooking meat is that the tough collagen in the meat's connective tissue converts into gelatin without the meat's protein denaturing to a point at which the meat juices are squeezed out, which can leave the texture dry and tough. The lower temperature used for vegetables allows them to be fully cooked while maintaining a crisp texture that is uniform all the way through.

Other general benefits of sous-vide cooking include the following: the food is cooked in and retains its own juices; the food does not oxidize as it is sealed in an airtight bag; the ambient temperatures mean that foods maintain more of their nutrients; foods can be cooked for long periods of time without being over-cooked, as the core temperature will not exceed the water-bath's set temperature; and foods stored in airtight bags can be kept refrigerated for longer periods before expiring.

The sous-vide method does have a couple of minor drawbacks, however. The first and most important is the health and safety issue of cooking meats at such low temperatures. This, coupled with the long periods required for foods to reach their full core temperature, can provide a perfect breeding ground for bacteria if the food is mishandled. Meat cooked for longer in order to tenderize it must reach

The sous-vide technique is an innovative and delicious way to prepare salmon (see recipe page 84).

a temperature of at least 131°F (55°C) within four hours and then be kept at that temperature in order to pasteurize the meat.

The second drawback is the absence of browning (the Maillard reaction), a process that creates additional flavors and textures. The Maillard reaction occurs at temperatures above boiling point and therefore is not achieved using sous-vide cooking. To compensate for this, chefs will sear the meat in a very hot skillet to ensure that only the outside of the meat is cooked either before or after cooking it in the water-bath.

### Equipment and Ingredients

1. Vacuum-packing machine

    Removes the air out of a bag or container producing a vacuum, which reduces volume for storage and keeps the items better protected from oxidization. Professional models are very expensive, so stick with a domestic model. The main drawback with these is that you cannot vacuum-pack liquids in the vacuum-packing bags (3), but there are ways of getting around this, which are detailed later on in this chapter (see Tips, page 83).

2. Water-bath

    A water-bath is a temperature-controlled water basin, which will cook foods at a set temperature for hours on end. They are very easy to use. In this book we have used a water-bath manufactured by Clifton Food Range, a company that produces excellent-quality equipment that is both accurate and durable, as well as being aesthetically pleasing.

## Preparation and Cooking Times

Set the temperature on the water-bath and allow it to come to the full set temperature before placing the food inside — note that the temperature may drop slightly once the food is placed inside (this will depend on the food's starting temperature and the size of the water-bath), but will soon return to the set temperature.

Vacuum-pack your ingredients — note that not all vacuum-packing machines are capable of vacuum-packing liquids and not all vacuum-packing bags are meant to be used in a water-bath; some are produced just for storage purposes.

Once the water-bath has reached the full set temperature, place the vacuum-packed food inside and set a timer or make a note of the time at which it should be removed.

For cooking times and temperatures, refer to the sous-vide reference guide at www.sousvidesupreme.com.

## Tips

1. Experiment by vacuum-packing foods with liquids (juice, jus, stock, oil and alcohol, for example), herbs and aromatics, which will cook with the natural juices of the ingredient to create even more complex and interesting flavors.

2. If your vacuum-packing machine cannot vacuum-pack liquids, either refrigerate or freeze the liquids until they are solid (meat jus and some fats will firm up in a refrigerator; other liquids can be frozen).

3. Be aware not to over-season or over-spice foods in the vacuum-packing bag as the flavors will intensify over the prolonged cooking time.

4. Use a digital probe thermometer to measure the core temperature of the cooked food.

5. If the food is not going to be consumed immediately after cooking then place it — still vacuum-packed — in an ice bath to rapidly reduce its temperature to 41°F (5°C) in order to reduce the risk of bacterial growth.

6. Don't cook frozen meats using this technique as the time required for them to reach a safe core temperature may be too long and cause bacterial growth to occur.

Egg yolks prepared using the sous-vide method and then deep fried in fine breadcrumbs make wonderful tapas.

# SOUS-VIDE SALMON

**INGREDIENTS**

1 lb 5 oz (600 g)
   salmon fillet
½ tsp (2 ml) olive oil
¾ tsp (3 g) salt
¾ tsp (3 g) superfine sugar
zest of 1 lemon

**Serves 4**

1. Remove the skin from the salmon fillet and discard. Divide the fillet into 4 equal portions.

2. Gently rub the salmon with olive oil, season with the salt and sugar and sprinkle the lemon zest on the cut side (not the skin side).

3. Place the salmon in a vacuum-packing bag and seal it. Place the bag in a pre-heated water-bath set at 127°F (53°C) and leave it to cook for 15–20 minutes, depending on the thickness of the salmon pieces.

4. Take the salmon out of the water-bath and remove it from the sealed bag. Serve a perfectly cooked piece of salmon.

## Serving suggestions

- Salmon with zucchini strips and fennel fluid gel (pictured opposite)

- Salmon with curly kale and *sauce vierge*

- Salmon with *pomme purée* and squid ink sauce

- Salmon with raisin and cilantro cous cous

# SOUS-VIDE OXTAIL

## INGREDIENTS

8 oxtails

⅔ cup (150 ml) red wine

1½ cups (350 ml)
   beef stock

2 bay leaves

3 juniper berries

2 cloves of garlic

salt

**Serves 4**

1. Sear the oxtails in a hot skillet until they have an even, golden-brown appearance.

2. Remove the oxtails from the skillet then pour in the red wine. Bring to a boil, reduce the heat and simmer for a couple of minutes, then remove from the heat.

3. Combine all the ingredients, then split them equally between 2 vacuum-packing bags and seal the bags. If your vacuum-packing machine cannot vacuum-pack liquids, see the Tips section on page 83.

4. Place the sealed bags into a pre-heated water-bath set at 176°F (80°C) and cook for 10 hours.

5. Take the oxtails out of the water-bath and remove them from the sealed bag, reserving the cooking juices.

6. Strain the cooking juices using a sieve and pour them into a saucepan. Bring them to a boil, reduce the heat to a simmer and reduce the juices.

7. Once the cooking juices are reduced just enough to coat the back of a spoon, add the oxtails to the saucepan and baste them. Season to taste and serve.

## Serving suggestions

- Oxtail with roasted potatoes and seasonal vegetables (pictured opposite)

- Oxtail burger (flake the meat off the bone between steps 5 and 6)

- Oxtail with pappardelle pasta, parsley and Parmesan

# SOUS-VIDE PUMPKIN

**INGREDIENTS**

1 small pumpkin
salt
1 oz (28 g) butter

**Serves 4**

1. Cut the pumpkin in half, remove the seeds and cut into wedges, then remove the skin from the wedges.

2. Dice the pumpkin flesh into 1 inch (2.5 cm) cubes and sprinkle with salt. Place the pumpkin cubes and butter into a vacuum-packing bag and seal.

3. Place the bag into a pre-heated water-bath set at 176°F (80°C) and cook until the pumpkin is tender — it should take 2–4 hours, depending on the variety of pumpkin and the size of the cubes. A ½ inch (1.3 cm) cube of pumpkin will take approximately 4 hours.

4. Remove the pumpkin from the water-bath and place the contents of the bag into a blender. Blend until you have a smooth consistency.

## Serving suggestions

- Pumpkin purée (add vegetable stock and cream during step 2, then strain through a fine sieve), with seared scallops and black pudding (pictured opposite)

- Pumpkin mash with honey-roasted chicken and crispy bacon (rather than blending the pumpkin in step 4, simply crush it into a mash)

- Pumpkin, sage and honey soup (add some sage to the vacuum-packing bag in step 2, then add vegetable stock, honey to taste and a touch of cream for richness during step 4 then strain through a fine sieve)

# TECHNIQUE 5: TRANSGLUTAMINASE

Transglutaminase is a naturally occurring enzyme with the ability to bond animal tissue. Its less technical name among chefs is "meat glue," given that this is its main function in the kitchen (although it has other uses in commercial food processing). Transglutaminase doesn't directly change the flavor or texture of food, it simply binds animal tissue together. This allows innovative chefs to create new and interesting combinations, a popular example being American chef Wylie Dufresne's shrimp pasta dish, in which he makes the pasta purely out of shrimp. Transglutaminase can bond meats of the same kind or different kinds together, for example scallops could be bonded together or they could even be bonded to bacon.

## Brief Background

Transglutaminase was first identified in 1959. Initially it was expensive to produce, however by the late 1980s researchers at a Japanese company called Ajinomoto — a large producer of both transglutaminase and monosodium glutamate (MSG) — discovered a simpler way to produce large quantities, making it much cheaper.

Transglutaminase has been used in commercial food processing over the years for a diverse range of products, including deli meat (for binding), yogurt (to thicken and reduce water leakage), as well as processed cheese, pasta and bread (for texture). It has only recently been adopted by chefs in restaurants, and as mentioned it is typically used to bind meats.

## The Science Behind the Technique

Although it may sound a little foreign to be using an enzyme in the kitchen, it is important to note the role enzymes have played in the cooking process over thousands of years. Examples include the rennet enzyme used to curdle milk in the cheese-making process; the enzymes — including yeast — used to break down the sugars in the fermentation of beer, and for viscosity control (in beer and other malted liquor); and the enzymes papain and bromelain (derived from papaya and pineapples), which are the two most commonly used meat tenderizers.

Transglutaminase has several benefits: first of all it can allow meat mixtures to be bound without casings or the use of egg (a plus for those with allergies); it can be used to make interesting new dishes like meat spaghetti (nothing new to anyone familiar with Asian fish balls); uniform portions can be achieved by binding meats and then cutting them into equal portions; and finally it can be used to make novel combinations like chicken-steak fillets.

## Tips

1. Once the food is "glued," avoid disturbing it so as not to break the bonds until they have set.

2. Think carefully about which meats to bind. Different meats require different cooking times, for example a scallop will over-cook if glued to a thick piece of chicken.

3. Store opened pouches by wrapping tightly (vacuum packing is a good idea) and placing in the freezer (this slows down the enzyme's binding reaction until you are ready to use it again).

4. Cooked meats will bind together but the bond will not be as strong as when "gluing" raw meats together.

5. Try to get the "gluing" process done within 30 minutes, and if using a slurry discard any leftovers.

6. Don't bond warm meat inside any other type of food if it will be stored as this can lead to bacterial development.

7. Always use fresh meats to avoid bacterial development.

8. Limit any contact with your skin (wearing gloves is advisable) and do not inhale or allow it to come into contact with your eyes.

## Preparation and Cooking Times

The quantity of transglutaminase required will usually be between 0.75 percent and 1 percent of the total weight of the food.

Transglutaminase comes in powder form and there are two ways of applying it. The first is to lightly sprinkle (dust) the powder evenly onto the surface of the meat using a fine sieve (pictured left) or a pepper shaker. The second is to mix with water

(a slurry), using two parts water to one part transglutaminase, and then brush this onto the meat. If making a slurry, discard any leftovers that will not be used within 30 minutes of its preparation. Note that only the surface which will be "glued" needs to be coated.

Once the surfaces of the meat are coated, press them together, removing any air bubbles, wrap with plastic wrap or vacuum pack and allow to rest for at least 3 hours in a refrigerator for the bonding process to take place.

Alternatively, there is a process known as heat setting which sets the bonds at a much faster rate (between 5 and 20 minutes). The temperature required is between 122°F (50°C) and 136°F (58°C), and the food must reach a core temperature of 131°F (55°C). This is most accurately done by immersing the transglutaminase-mixed food into a water-bath (as much more precise and stable temperatures can be attained) and leaving it in the water-bath until its core temperature has reached the bonding level for 5 minutes. Once this has been achieved the food can be removed and cooked to serving temperature.

### Equipment and Ingredients

1. Transglutiminase

   Comes in powder form and is available to buy from modernistpantry.com.

2. Wire Sieve

   The easiest way to dust the meat with transglutimanese is using a wire sieve.

3. Brush

   Alternative to dusting is applying a 2:1 tranglutimanese:water slurry mixture using a brush.

# SEA BREAM STUFFED WITH SUN-DRIED TOMATO PESTO

**INGREDIENTS**

2 sea bream fillets

5 tbsp (74 ml) sun-dried tomato pesto

transglutaminase slurry

**Serves 1**

1. Place the two fillets skin-side down on a clean cutting board and spread the sun-dried tomato pesto onto the center of one of the fillets.

2. Brush the slurry onto the flesh of the fish and place the flesh sides of the two fillets together. Wrap tightly in plastic wrap or vacuum pack and leave to rest for 2 hours in the refrigerator.

3. Remove the fish from the plastic wrap/vacuum pack, then pan fry, grill or bake the fish as you wish. Keep in mind that this is now one thick fillet so it will take longer to cook all the way through.

## Serving suggestions

- Pan-fried sea bream stuffed with sun-dried tomato pesto, served with saffron rice and seasonal vegetables (pictured opposite)

- Baked sea bream stuffed with sun-dried tomatoes and baked mushrooms with buffalo mozzarella

- Grilled sea bream stuffed with basil pesto (substitute basil pesto in step 1) and grilled Mediterranean vegetables

TRANSGLUTAMINASE

# SPICY SHRIMP SAUSAGES

## INGREDIENTS

1 lb (454 g) peeled raw
  shrimp
¾ tsp (3 ml) smoked
  paprika
¾ tsp (3 ml) cayenne
  pepper
1 tsp (5 ml) salt
1¼ oz (35 g) caramelized
  diced shallot
¼ tsp (1 ml) thyme
¾ tsp (3 ml) garlic paste
1 tbsp (15 ml)
  Worcestershire sauce
1 tsp (5 ml)
  transglutaminase

**Serves 4**

1. Purée half the shrimp with all of the ingredients except the transglutaminase in a food processor.

2. Chop the remaining shrimp into medium-sized chunks.

3. Combine all the ingredients except the transglutaminase together in a mixing bowl.

4. Sprinkle the transglutaminase a third at a time over the mix and fold in, making sure it is equally distributed.

5. Place the mixture on a sheet of plastic wrap and roll to form a cylindrical "sausage" shape. Place the "sausage" in the refrigerator overnight to set.

6. Vacuum pack the "sausage" and place into a water bath pre-heated to 136°F (58°C) for 20 minutes.

7. Remove the "sausage" from the bath and immediately chill in an ice bath for 20 minutes.

8. Remove the "sausage" from the vacuum-packing bag and remove the plastic wrap. Slice into portions and in a hot pan sear with a little olive oil.

## Serving suggestions

- Spicy shrimp sausage canapés with chili mango salsa (pictured opposite)

- Spicy shrimp sausage with seafood pasta

- Spicy shrimp sausage with Thai red curry and coconut rice

# BACON-WRAPPED SCALLOPS

**INGREDIENTS**

6 large scallops

6 strips of bacon

transglutaminase slurry

**Serves 2**

1. Remove the roe from the scallops, then wash and gently pat them dry.

2. Trim the bacon so that each piece wraps around a scallop once and is the right height. Lay the trimmed pieces of bacon on a cutting board and brush with the slurry.

3. Place each scallop on the slurry-brushed side of a piece of bacon, then roll the bacon around each of the scallops.

4. Plastic wrap each bacon scallop individually and leave to rest in the refrigerator for 2 hours.

5. Pre-heat the oven to 428°F (220°C). Remove the plastic wrap and place the scallops in a hot skillet with olive oil and cook both scallop sides until they are a beautiful golden color.

6. Once both the scallop sides are done, place the scallops in the pre-heated oven for around 5 minutes, depending on the size of the scallops.

## Serving suggestions

- Bacon-wrapped scallop canapés (pictured opposite)

- Scallops wrapped in bacon with black pudding and pumpkin purée

- Pan-fried monkfish with scallops wrapped in bacon and a red wine jus

TRANSGLUTAMINASE

# TECHNIQUE 6: COLD GELS & FLUID GELS

Cold gels have become increasingly popular within the culinary world. Initially used only for desserts, they have now found a place among starters and sometimes even main courses. This has been largely due to the fact that chefs are now more aware of the wide range of gelling agents and their diverse applications and properties.

A large number of gelling agents are available, however for the purpose of this chapter we will focus on gelatin, carrageenan and xanthan gum, as they demonstrate a diverse range of uses and properties that will provide a solid understanding of the fundamentals of gels.

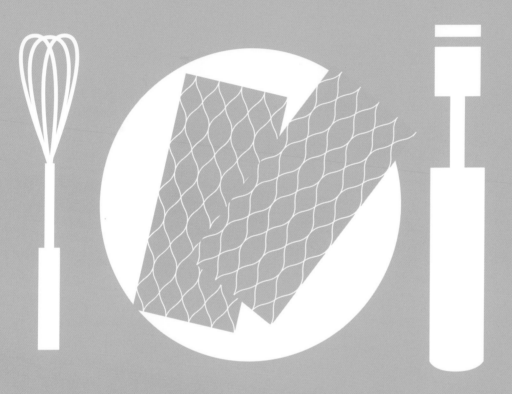

# GELLING AGENTS

## Gelatin

Gelatin is probably the most familiar gel to home cooks and professional chefs alike. It is extracted from the collagen of bones or skin (mostly from pigs and calves). Gelatin first came to culinary prominence in the 17th century and rapidly became a commonly used ingredient by both chefs and the food manufacturing industry, where it is used in jelly, gummy candy, marshmallows, mousses, desserts, ice cream and yogurt.

**Properties:** Gelatin makes flexible gels that range in firmness depending on the quantity used. It is a thermo-reversible gel with good flavor release and a relatively clear appearance. It is generally very versatile and pH tolerant so it can be used to gel juices, alcohols and dairy products. A big advantage of gelatin is that it can be dissolved into a small amount of a liquid and then mixed into the remaining liquid, meaning the entire solution does not have to be heated. Its limitations are that it cannot be frozen and that it breaks under shearing.

**Using Gelatin:** Gelatin comes in the form of a powder or brittle translucent sheets. It is used in concentrations of around 1 percent to 1.5 percent. When using gelatin sheets a minimum of four sheets per four cups (1 liter) are required for a soft gel and a maximum of 20 sheets per four cups (1 liter) for harder, more chewy gels.

Soak gelatin sheets in cold water for several minutes in order to hydrate them, a process known as "blooming." Once the sheets have softened, remove from the water and squeeze out the excess water. Then add to a hot liquid (over 140°F/60°C) and stir to dissolve. Once the gelatin is dissolved, pour into a mold and leave to set in the refrigerator (at around 39°F/4°C) for about 3 hours. If using gelatin powder, skip the "blooming" step and mix directly into the hot water.

## Tips

1. Make sure you hydrate the gelling agents properly, most of them have their own method which when applied will produce optimal results.

2. Experiment with proportions, the difference between using a 1 percent or 2 percent concentration of a gelling agent will usually be quite noticeable and yield a different texture and mouth feel.

3. Experiment with combining gelling agents in different proportions, the resulting jellies will vary greatly depending on the proportions and type of gelling agents mixed.

The gelling agent iota carrageenan is used in this chocolate milk gel recipe to create a good freeze–thaw stability (see page 112 for base recipe).

Adding xanthan gum to a fruit punch will thicken the mix in just two hours, allowing you to add pieces of chopped fruit that will appear suspended in the drink.

### Carrageenan

There are three types of carrageenan: kappa, lambda and iota (this chapter will focus on kappa and iota), all of which are extracted from "Irish Moss" seaweed. Carrageenan has been in use for several hundred years; one of its earliest uses was as a thickener in milk-based puddings. It has since been used by the food manufacturing industry in sliced ham, glazes, ice cream, sterilized milk, soy milk, sauces and of course milk-based desserts.

**Properties:** Kappa carrageenan makes firm, brittle gels which have poor freeze–thaw stability and will break under shearing; iota carrageenan forms very elastic gels which have good freeze–thaw stability and re-form after shearing.

Both are thermo-reversible: they must be heated to 158°F (70°C) or above, and when cooled they begin to gel at temperatures ranging between 104°F (40°C) and 140°F (60°C).

The appearance of the gels are hazy (less so in the presence of sugar), they have good flavor release and will lose viscosity and gel strength in solutions below pH values of about 4.3. Both iota and kappa are commonly used in milk-based gels and desserts as they are effective at concentrations as low as 0.3 percent.

Carrageenan gels are stable at room temperature and can be re-melted by heating to between 41°F (5°C) and 68°F (20°C) above the gelling temperature; when cooled again the solution will re-gel.

**Using Carrageenan:** Carrageenan is commonly used in concentrations of between 0.75 percent and 1 percent in water (including juices) and 0.35 percent and 0.5 percent in milk to form solid gels, and in lower concentrations for fluid gels.

Disperse the carrageenan in a cold liquid (milk is best, but other liquids such as juices or even beer also work) using a hand-held immersion blender (any lumps produced while dispersing carrageenan reduce the development of full viscosity or gel strength). Bring the liquid to a boil, pour into the desired mold, then leave to set at room temperature or in the refrigerator.

## Xanthan Gum

Xanthan gum, also called xanthana, is produced through the fermentation of glucose or sucrose by the *Xanthomonas campestris* bacterium. It acts as a thickener, adding viscosity to the liquids in which it is dispersed. It does not form solid gels, but creates solutions which look like gels when still, yet which pour easily when agitated. It is used by the food manufacturing industry in the production of sauces, as an egg yolk replacement (for thickening), in batters, baked goods, pie fillings, dairy products and vinaigrette-style dressings (especially dressings with pieces suspended in them). It is also used by chefs to create "fluid gels."

**Properties:** Xanthan gum is very versatile and works well across a range of pH levels. It is heat tolerant, salt tolerant, can be dispersed in hot or cold liquids and although it will not dissolve directly in alcohol, xanthan gum solutions are compatible with alcohol. It is useful as an emulsifier, as an additive to reduce syneresis and its ability to trap air bubbles well makes it useful for foams. Finally, xanthan gum is thixotropic, meaning that it thins upon shearing

Gelatin comes in the form of translucent sheets. When softened in cold water and squeezed of excess water, they can be dissolved in hot liquid to create a flexible gel used most commonly in mousses and desserts.

then thickens up again when left to rest.

It is known to reduce ice crystal formation and is actually strengthened by the freeze–thaw cycle.

**Using Xanthan Gum:** Xanthan gum is typically used in concentrations of between 0.5 percent and 1 percent (although it can go lower).

Disperse the xanthan gum in a liquid (hot or cold). This is most easily achieved using a hand-held immersion blender (if it is not well dispersed it will form swollen lumps in the solution). The solution will be ready to use as soon as this hydration process is complete.

### Equipment and Ingredients

1.  Gelatin

    An animal product extracted from the collagen of bones or skin. Gelatin is commonly used by home cooks and professional chefs alike to produce jellies and firm mousses.

2.  Xanthan gum (E415)

    Made by the fermentation of sugars by the bacterium *Xanthomonas campestris*. Used by food manufacturers as an emulsifier, thickener and stabilizer, it is most commonly used by modernist chefs as a thickener, to add body to a liquid and form fluid gels.

3.  Carrageenan (E407)

    A natural substance extracted from red seaweed also called "Irish Moss." Used in food manufacturing for gelling, thickening and stabilizing, it is most commonly used as a gelling agent in the modern chef's kitchen. There are three types of carrageenan: kappa, lambda and iota.

4.  Hand-held immersion blender

    These are also known as stick blenders. They are a must-have gadget for any amateur chef and a vital tool for a budding molecular gastronomist. It is basically an open-ended hand blender that allows you to mix and blend ingredients in a bowl. They are great for mixing gelling agents into liquids and creating fantastic light foams and airs.

5.  Whisk

    A whisk can be useful when dissolving sheets of gelatin in hot liquid as it will speed up the thickening process.

# CRAB MOUSSE

## INGREDIENTS

5 oz (142 g) white crab
  meat
²/₃ cup (150 ml) crab
  consommé
¹/₅ cup (50 ml) mayonnaise
1 tbsp (15ml)
  Worcestershire sauce
3 drops Tabasco sauce
3 gelatin leaves
2 tbsp (30 ml) warm water
²/₃ cup (150 ml) whipped
  cream
chopped chives
1¹/₃ tbsp (20 ml) lemon
  juice
salt and black pepper, to
  taste

**Serves 2**

1. Combine the white crab meat, consommé, mayonnaise, lemon juice and sauces in a food processor and mix to a smooth paste.

2. Soak the gelatin leaves in cold water, and once softened dissolve into the warm water.

3. Transfer the crab paste into a mixing bowl and fold in the whipped cream and chopped chives, then season to taste.

4. Add the gelatin water and mix well.

5. Portion into plastic wrap-lined ramekins or molds and leave in the refrigerator to set.

### Serving suggestions

- Crab mousse served with mango, chili and watercress salad (pictured opposite)

- Crab mousse and cucumber salad with truffle vinaigrette

- Crab mousse with diced mango and wholegrain mustard dressing

# CHOCOLATE MILK GEL

## INGREDIENTS

¹/₅ cup (50 ml) melted
    chocolate
⁴/₅ cup (200 ml) milk
0.03 oz (0.9 g) iota
    carrageenan

**Serves 2**

1. Mix the melted chocolate and milk together.

2. Mix in the Iota using your hand-held immersion blender until completely dispersed.

3. Heat the mixture to 185°F (85°C).

4. Pour the mixture into a mold(s) and place in the refrigerator to set.

5. Once set, blend the gel in a jug blender to create a chocolate milk fluid gel.

## Serving suggestions

- Chocolate gel-covered strawberries (dip strawberries into the warm chocolate mix after step 3, then refrigerate) (pictured opposite)

- Chocolate gel topped with raspberries and mint dessert canapé

- Peanut butter brownies with a fluid chocolate gel

# XANTHAN GUM USES

### Fruit punch suspension

Using a hand-held immersion blender, add around 0.2 percent xanthan gum by weight to a fruit punch mix of your liking. Pass the mix through a fine chinois and leave to rest for 2 hours. The mix should be thick enough to allow you to incorporate pieces of chopped fruit (or fruit-flavored caviar) that will be suspended in the drink (pictured opposite).

### Thickening milkshakes

Using a hand-held immersion blender, add around 0.1 percent xanthan gum by weight to your milkshake. It will instantly turn your "milky" consistency milkshake into a thick shake.

### Fruit fluid gel

Using a hand-held immersion blender, add around 0.5 percent xanthan gum by weight to a fruit juice. This will thicken it up enough so that you can spoon it onto your plate.

# TECHNIQUE 7: HEAT-TOLERANT GELS

A phenomenon which picked up popularity in modernist
kitchens is the use of warm gels. This is in part due to the fact
that it confuses our senses; we expect gels to be cold because
we are used to jelly (typically made of gelatin), and therefore,
foods with a gel-like texture, which are warm, seem somewhat
incongruent. There are a number of gelling agents available that
exhibit various levels of heat-tolerant characteristics; however, for
the purpose of this chapter, agar agar, methyl cellulose and gellan
gum have been selected as they demonstrate a diverse range of
uses and properties which will provide a solid understanding of the
fundamentals of gels.

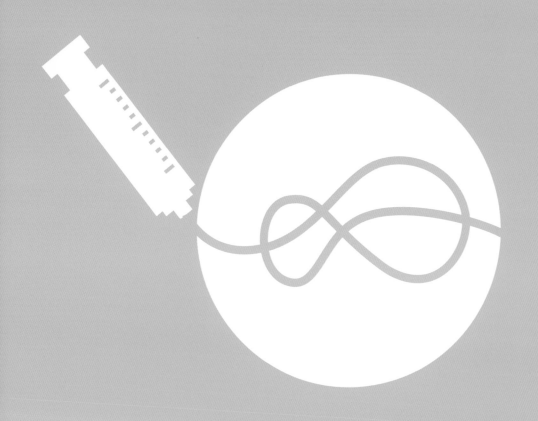

# GELLING AGENTS

### Agar Agar

Agar agar, also called agar, is a gelling agent derived from red algae. It has been used for centuries by the Japanese and other Far Eastern countries, mainly as a gelling agent in desserts. It is available in most Asian food stores and has even found its way into many large supermarkets.

Despite its widespread use throughout the Far East, agar gained greater culinary prominence in Western kitchens after Chef Ferran Adrià of El Bulli restaurant in Spain used it to make jellies which could be served warm, highlighting one of its most unique properties: that once set, agar gels will not melt until a temperature of around 185°F (85°C) is reached.

**Properties**: Agar is only soluble in hot liquids, which must reach a temperature of 194°F (90°C). It forms firm gels which are thermo-reversible and set at room temperature, it is tolerant to a wide range of pH levels and can be used in sweet and salty liquids alike. Agar breaks under shearing (which can form very good fluid gels), is not freeze-thaw stable and has moderately good flavor release, although the agar itself does interfere slightly with the actual flavor of the liquid being gelled.

**Using Agar Agar**: Agar comes in various forms, as a powder, translucent sticks, or flakes. It is used in concentrations of between 0.5 percent and 2 percent. To hydrate, bring the liquid to be gelled to a boil and whisk in the agar. Once it has dissolved and the solution has a smooth consistency, remove from the heat and pour into a mold. Leave the solution to set either at room temperature or in the refrigerator for around 15 to 30 minutes.

### Methyl Cellulose

Methyl cellulose is a chemical compound derived from cellulose (the structural cells of living plants). It is a fascinating gelling agent as unlike other gelling agents it turns into a solid gel upon heating. As well as being a gelling agent, it is also a good thickener and emulsifier

Agar agar mixed with Parmesan is used in the making of gel noodles (see recipe page 126).

and is widely used by the food and cosmetics industries in everything from shampoo, toothpaste and liquid soap to baked goods (mainly pie fillings so they don't spill out during cooking), ice cream and sauces.

For chefs, methyl cellulose presents the opportunity to create interesting new culinary delights; it has been used to make hot mozzarella sheets, hot gelled noodles and even hot ice cream (which melts as it cools).

**Properties**: It is important to note that there are several types of methyl cellulose: A, SG A, E, F and K. The A types (SG A and A) are methyl cellulose (MC). Types E, F and K are hydroxypropyl methyl cellulose (HPMC). Each type will have different properties in terms of viscosity, gelling temperature and gel characteristics.

Generally, methyl cellulose gels are thermo-reversible, have good flavor release and are soluble in cold liquids (although they can be added to hot liquids which must then be quickly chilled to below gelling temperature — this works well for types A and SG A). In addition, methyl cellulose gels set fast, have good freeze–thaw stability, are tolerant to a range of pH levels (2 to 13) and will break under shearing.

| Type | Gelling temperature | Gel characteristic |
|------|--------------------|--------------------|
| A | 122°F–131°F (50°C–55°C) | Firm gel |
| SG A | 100°F–111°F (38°C–44°C) | Firm, rigid gel |
| E | 136°F–147°F (58°C–64°C) | Semi-firm gel |
| F | 145°F–154°F (63°C–68°C) | Semi-firm gel |
| K | 158°F–194°F (70°C–90°C) | Soft gel |

**Using Methyl Cellulose:** Methyl cellulose comes in powder form and is used in concentrations of between 0.75 percent and 2 percent.

Bring the liquid to be gelled to a temperature above 131°F (55°C) (but not above 212°F [100°C], so a steady simmer is good). Whisk in the methyl cellulose, then remove the solution from the heat and place in an ice bath or add cold liquid to bring the temperature to below the gelling point. The solution should be mixed continuously as it cools to allow the methyl cellulose to fully dissolve. Avoid over-whisking as this can cause excess air bubbles. Leave the solution to rest for several hours (preferably overnight) as the methyl cellulose will hydrate as the solution cools.

Once the methyl cellulose has fully hydrated, the solution will thicken. To test whether it has hydrated properly, place a small quantity of the hydrated solution into simmering water and it will set into a gel.

Once the agar agar-Parmesan gel mix has set, the tubing is emptied gently with a syringe full of air to make the noodles (see recipe on page 126).

## Gellan Gum

Gellan gum, also called "gellan," is a gelling agent produced through the fermentation of *Sphingomonas elodea*, a type of bacteria that grows on an aquatic plant. It is unique as a gelling agent due to its high tolerance when heated; once set, the jelly can be heated to about 176°F (80°C) without melting (and even higher depending on the type of gellan used).

It is also used as a thickener, stabilizer and emulsifier, and low-acyl gellan can even be used for spherification in replacement of the sodium alginate (although this is much trickier as it is very sensitive to calcium, potassium and sodium salts). The food manufacturing industry uses gellan in baked goods, gummy candy, jellies, jams, sauces and dairy products.

**Properties:** There are two types of gellan: high-acyl and low-acyl. Each has its own distinct set of properties and gel characteristics.

Under shear, both gels will break and form excellent fluid gels. In addition it is important to note that a mixture of the two can result in very versatile gels which have the characteristics and properties of both high- and low-acyl gels. To achieve a texture which is roughly halfway between each type, a ratio of 75 percent low-acyl to 25 percent high-acyl would be used.

**Using Gellan Gum:** Gellan comes in powder form and is typically used in concentrations of between 0.1 percent and 1 percent. Simply bring the liquid to be gelled to a simmer and whisk in the gellan until it is dissolved. Remove from the heat, pour into a mold and leave to set in a refrigerator for 15 minutes to 1 hour.

| | High-acyl | Low-acyl |
|---|---|---|
| Gel characteristic | Flexible | Brittle |
| Solubility | Hot liquids | Hot and cold liquids |
| Gel appearance | Hazy | Clear |
| Flavor release | Good | Very good |
| Set temperature | 158°F–176°F (70°C–80°C) | 86°F–122°F (30°C–50°C) |
| Melting temperature | 158°F–176°F (70°C–80°C) | Does not melt |
| Thermo-reversible | Yes | No |
| Freeze–thaw stability | Stable | Not stable |
| Syneresis | Yes | No |
| pH tolerance | 3–10 | 4–10 |

Gellan gum needs to be whisked into simmering liquid and thoroughly combined to produce the best gel.

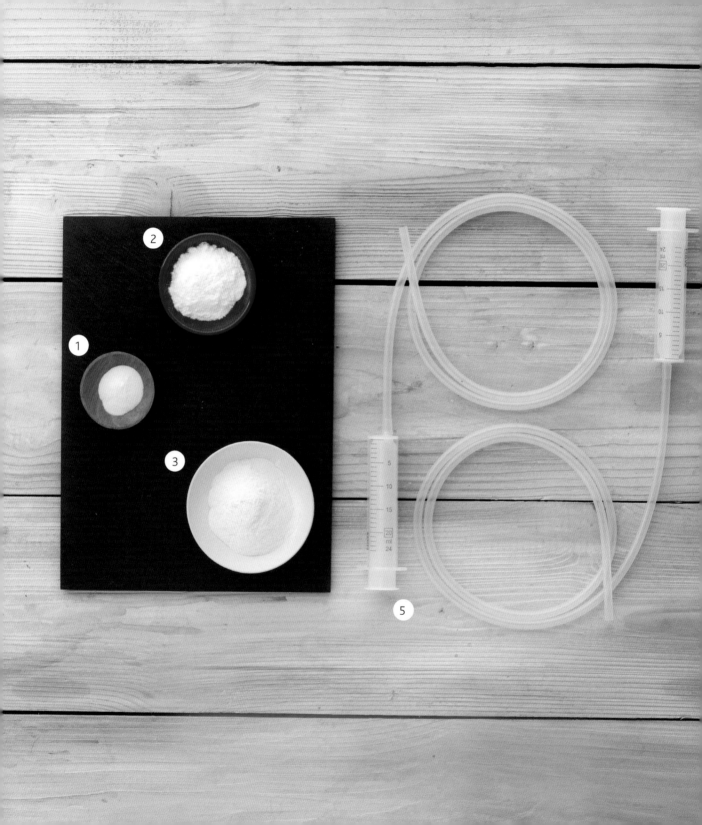

### Equipment and Ingredients

1.  Agar agar (E406)

    This is a gelling agent derived from red algae. It is most commonly used by chefs to make heat-tolerant gels which can be served up to temperatures of around 185°F (85°C).

2.  Methyl cellulose (E461)

    A synthetic compound made from cellulose. It is typically used as a thickener, stabilizer, emulsifier, gelling agent and binding agent. It is a particularly interesting gelling agent as it gels upon heating. This has inspired chefs to make dishes which include elements such as hot mozzarella sheets, hot gelled noodles and even hot ice cream — which melts as it cools.

3.  Gellan (E418)

    A gelling agent produced through the fermentation of *Sphingomonas elodea*, a type of bacteria that grows on an aquatic plant. It is unique as a gelling agent due to its high tolerance when heated; once set, the jelly can be heated to about 176°F (80°C) without melting.

4.  Whisk

    Essential for whisking agar agar, gellan or methyl cellulose into simmering liquids.

5.  Plastic syringe and plastic tubes

    Essential if making the Parmesan noodles on page 126.

# WARM PARMESAN NOODLES

## INGREDIENTS

⁴/₅ cup (200 ml) vegetable stock

7 oz (200 g) grated fresh Parmesan

0.22 oz (6.2 g) agar agar

**Serves 4**

1. Bring the stock to a boil, remove from the heat and add the Parmesan. Cover and set aside for 20 minutes. Strain through a fine chinois, reserving the liquid.

2. Bring the "Parmesan water" to a boil then reduce the heat. Whisk in the agar agar until completely dissolved, then remove from the heat.

3. Fill a syringe about half full with the Parmesan–agar mix and attach the plastic tube. Gently push the mix from the syringe through the plastic tube, leaving about 1 inch (2.5 cm) toward the end of the tube.

4. Immerse the filled tube in an ice bath and leave to chill for 2 minutes, or until the Parmesan mix has set to a jelly. Remove the tube from the ice bath and pat dry.

5. Fill an empty syringe with air and attach the tube containing the Parmesan jelly. Very gently press on the syringe in order to push the jelly out of the tube.

6. Repeat steps 3, 4 and 5 until you have used all the Parmesan mix. The noodles can be served immediately or stored in the refrigerator for up to 12 hours.

Remember: agar agar gels can withstand temperatures of up to around 185°F (85°C) before melting, so you can gently heat the noodles before serving.

## Serving suggestions

- Parmesan noodles with prosciutto, asparagus, poached quail egg and truffle foam (pictured opposite)

- Parmesan noodles served in a clear chicken consommé

# WARM VANILLA MOUSSE

**INGREDIENTS**

1 lb (454 g) clotted cream

$^1/_3$ cup (80 ml) honey

scrapings from 1 vanilla pod

$^2/_3$ cup (150 ml) water

0.38 oz (11 g) methyl
cellulose

**Serves 4**

1. Blend the clotted cream, honey and vanilla scrapings together in a blender.

2. Bring the water to a boil in a saucepan and whisk in the methyl cellulose.

3. Once the methyl cellulose has dissolved in the water, add to the blender and mix all the ingredients together until you have a homogenous mixture — do not over-blend as this will cause more air to become trapped in the mix.

4. Pour the mix into a bowl placed over an ice bath to reduce the temperature quickly, then place in the refrigerator overnight.

5. Bring a pot of water to a gentle simmer. Scoop up some of the vanilla cream mix and gently place it in the hot water. After a few seconds the mix will detach from the spoon or ladle. Leave to "cook" for approximately 2 minutes; the time will depend on the shape and size of your scoops.

6. Using a regular slotted spoon, gently remove the warm vanilla cream mousse from the hot water and serve.

Remember: methyl cellulose gels when heated and melts as it cools.

## Serving suggestions

- Warm vanilla mousse with baked apple, figs and honey (pictured opposite)

- Decorate your warm vanilla mousse as you would a banana split and call it a "hot vanilla ice cream"

# WARM FISH STOCK FETTUCCINE

## INGREDIENTS

5 saffron threads (optional)

1 cup (250 ml) unsalted fish consommé (clarified fish stock)

1 tsp (5 ml) gellan gum

**Serves 4**

1. Add the saffron threads (if using) to the fish consommé and bring to a boil.

2. Add the gellan gum using a hand-held immersion blender (don't over-aerate).

3. Strain the consommé mix using a chinois.

4. Pour the strained consommé mix onto a tray, tilting and moving it to allow the mix to spread evenly to form a thin, even sheet of gel, roughly $1/24$ inch (1 mm) in depth. (This is harder than it sounds as the gellan gum will begin to set almost instantly, so it may take a couple of attempts to get it right.) Leave it to set for a few minutes.

5. Gently peel the thin layer of gel off the tray and lay it flat on a clean cutting board.

6. Using a knife (and a ruler if you wish) cut the sheet into long strips roughly $1/4$ inch (6 mm) wide. The "pasta" strips are now ready to serve, or you can store them in the refrigerator for around 12 hours.

## Serving suggestions

- Shrimp seafood pasta with fish consommé fettuccine (pictured opposite)

- Grilled chicken with chicken consommé fettuccine and a light Alfredo sauce (use chicken consommé instead of fish consommé)

- Fish consommé fettuccine dressed with basil oil and a sprinkle of rock salt (or truffle salt)

# TECHNIQUE 8: DEHYDRATION

Dehydration is a technique in which foods are dried out at relatively low temperatures in order to remove the moisture, giving the dried ingredient a different texture and slightly modified flavor. Although it is an age-old preservation method, this technique has undergone somewhat of a renaissance with modernist chefs using this basic dehydration principle to create different textures and add interesting elements to dishes.

## Brief Background

Drying foods is a technique that has been around since the dawn of civilization and it served a very important purpose: food preservation. Until the advent of the refrigerator, drying, pickling and smoking were all vital to ensure there was food available all year round.

Nowadays preserved foods are enjoyed more for their textures and flavors, which are intensified by the dehydration process. Commonly produced dehydrated foods include dried fruits such as apricots and bananas, jerky (most commonly beef) and fruit roll-ups (also called fruit leather).

In recent years forward-thinking chefs have utilized the concept of dehydration as a means of introducing creative and interesting elements to dishes. Chef Ferran Adrià of El Bulli restaurant was one of the leaders in this, developing what is known as the Croquanter technique. Aside from this there are several other modern applications.

## Modern Dehydration Techniques

**The Croquanter Technique**: This involves dehydrating ingredients such as yogurt and fruit purées into geometrically shaped crispy sheets. These are used to add texture and flavor to a dish and also serve as a great garnish for plating.

**Powders and Soil:** This involves drying fruits and vegetables until all the moisture has been removed, then grinding them into either a coarse or fine powder form. Apart from adding an extra texture to the dish, they add flavor and are great for sprinkling on a plate for visual appeal.

**Dried Foams**: Meringues are technically a form of dried foam, however in this context the term relates to foams made from water-based liquids (vegetable or fruit juices) that have methyl cellulose and xanthan gum added. The mixed solution is then dehydrated to form a flavored crispy foam. As with the previous two methods, adding texture, flavor and visual appeal is the main purpose of this technique, although it is also a great way of making eggless meringues for those with allergies.

## Tips

1. For even results, turn the food and rotate the trays while the food is drying (this does not apply to foams).

2. If drying fruits or vegetables, test how far along the process is by tearing a piece in half. If there are moisture beads along the tear, it is not dry enough.

3. Dried food absorbs moisture from the air so the storage container must be airtight; plastic containers, glass jars and plastic freezer bags all work. Store the containers of dried food in a cool, dark, dry place at room temperature.

## Preparation and Cooking Times

Drying food in a regular domestic oven can be done, however it is very difficult to obtain good results and isn't very energy efficient. Most domestic ovens do not maintain the uniform level of heat that is required for the dehydration process. If you do choose to use your oven, set it at the lowest temperature and keep the door propped

open for air circulation, otherwise the oven will become humid and this will disturb the whole process.

The best results will always be obtained using an electric food dehydrator. These can be purchased for around $60 in the United States. They are energy efficient and will provide much more consistent results. They are also a great means of making delicious healthy snacks like dried fruits and meat jerky.

Dehydration is a lengthy process and will take several hours — up to 48 hours — to achieve the right results, so patience is required and preparing the dehydrated items ahead of time is a must. Once dehydrated, foods should be stored in airtight containers until ready to be served, so as to avoid the moisture in the air and maintain their crispy texture.

**Equipment and Ingredients**

1. Food dehydrator

   As the name suggests, this piece of equipment comes with the sole purpose of drying foods out at low temperatures over a period of many hours. An extremely simple piece of equipment to use — all you have to do is plug it in and set the temperature — it can be used to dehydrate fruits, vegetables and meats, which all make great snacks.

2. Teflon mat or parchment paper

   Either of these will work. The main purpose is to give foods a base to rest on as they are placed in the food dehydrator. Most dehydrators have perforated trays, so liquids or gels will not work.

3. Piping bag

   Essential for creating the Eggless Cranberry Meringues on page 141.

# DRIED-OLIVE SOIL

**INGREDIENTS USED**

Pitted black olives

**Serves 4**

1. Dry the olives with paper towel then place them in a dehydrator tray.

2. Dehydrate at 150°F (65°C) for 24 hours or until crunchy. If using an oven, set it to the minimum temperature possible and dry the olives for about 18 to 24 hours, leaving the oven door open about 2 inches (5 cm). Make sure you will be home for the entire duration so as not to leave the oven unattended. Taste for crunchiness during the dehydration process.

3. Grind the dried olives coarsely using a food processor.

## Serving suggestions

- Pecorino mousse topped with olive soil and baby basil (pictured opposite)

- Sprinkle olive soil over buffalo mozzarella, basil and cherry tomato salad

- Serve as a condiment/seasoning with meat or fish

# EGGLESS CRANBERRY MERINGUES

## INGREDIENTS

1⅕ cups (300 ml)
  cranberry juice
3½ oz (100 g) superfine
  sugar
0.25 oz (7 g) methyl
  cellulose
0.06 oz (1.7 g) xanthan
  gum

**Serves 6**

1. Combine the cranberry juice and sugar in a saucepan, bring to a simmer and heat until the sugar has dissolved.

2. Pour the cranberry juice into the bowl of a food mixer, add the methyl cellulose and disperse using a hand-held immersion blender.

3. Once the methyl cellulose has dissolved into the juice, add the xanthan gum, also dispersing using a hand-held immersion blender.

4. Place the bowl back in the mixer and, using the whisk attachment, mix on a medium speed until stiff peaks form.

5. Place the whipped mix into a piping bag and pipe out bite-sized amounts of the mix onto dehydrator mats or parchment paper.

6. Place in a dehydrator set at around 150°F (65°C) for 6 hours or until crunchy.

### Serving suggestion

- Cranberry meringues with lime mascarpone filling (pictured opposite)

- Beetroot meringues with a goat cheese filling

- Lemon meringues with a cranberry filling

# MANGO CRISPS

**INGREDIENTS**

3 mangoes or 7 oz (200 g)
mango purée

**Serves 6**

1. If using whole mangoes, remove the mango flesh and blend in a food processor until very smooth. If mangoes are not in season you could buy mango purée or use any other fruit.

2. Spread the purée onto a dehydrator mat or parchment paper to a thickness of around a quarter of an inch (6 mm). The more evenly you spread the purée the better your results will be.

3. Place in a dehydrator set at around 130°F (55°C) for approximately 8 to 10 hours. The crisps are ready once the mango purée has become brittle and there are no visible moist spots.

**Serving suggestion**

- Mango crisps with coconut cream (pictured opposite)

- Passion fruit crisps

- Strawberry crisps

# TECHNIQUE 9: RAPID INFUSION

The name of this technique makes it sound remarkably more technical than it really is. In short, it is used to infuse the flavor of porous ingredients (such as coffee beans, fruit peel or herbs) into a liquid (water, oil or alcohol) within minutes. Rapid infusion has been used in a wide variety of ways by chefs and mixologists alike.

## Brief Background

Using traditional methods, flavors are infused into liquids in one of two ways: by heating the liquid and then adding the infusion ingredient (hot infusion), or by adding the infusion ingredient to the cold liquid and then leaving it to infuse for a number of days (cold infusion).

More recently Dave Arnold, Director of Culinary Technology at the French Culinary Institute in New York, developed what is known as the rapid infusion technique. This involves using an iSi whipper (with nitrous oxide or carbon dioxide gas chargers) to create cold infusions in a matter of minutes.

## The Science Behind the Technique

Hot infusions are effective. However, the downside is that the application of heat to the liquid can alter its flavor. Take alcohol: it is a good solvent, but its volatility means that once it is heated many of its properties are lost. The same goes for extra-virgin olive oil: its distinctive and delicate flavor can be significantly altered when heated, hence it is mostly used for salad dressings or cold preparations. These ingredients can of course be infused using cold infusion, the downside being that this can take a number of days.

Depending on the ingredient that is to be infused, both traditional methods also run the risk of infusing more than just the main flavor characteristics. Examples of this include the "heat" from peppers and "bitterness" from fruit peel — although these are not the flavors that are meant to be extracted, they are sometimes infused into the liquid as well.

Rapid infusion works by using the pressure that is built up in the iSi whipper to force the liquid into the infusion ingredient. Once the pressure is released the liquids are pushed out of the infusion ingredient along with flavor molecules, which then dissipate into the liquid.

Most cold infusion recipes use nitrous oxide gas chargers, as nitrous oxide does not leave behind any noticeable flavor, whereas carbon dioxide gas chargers will leave a carbonated flavor, which is undesirable in most cases.

An iSi whipper is used to create the Instant Lemon-Infused Olive Oil on page 154.

**Equipment and Ingredients**

1. iSi Whipper

   Sometimes called an espuma, this is basically the professional chef's equivalent of a reusable whipped cream canister. You can reuse them with different liquids, gels and solids to produce a whole range of creams, foams and infusions. The iSi Whipper comes with a funnel lid-top (4) that is useful for adding ingredients to the canister.

2. $N_2O$ and $CO_2$ gas cartridges

   These can be used to make airy concoctions, or even fizzy ones. Carbon dioxide gas chargers are more suited to carbonation; for foams, stick with nitrous oxide chargers.

3. Sieve

   It is important to use a very fine sieve when carrying out this technique. iSi produce a great one that fits perfectly into their accompanying funnel.

### Preparation and Cooking Times

Pour liquid (water, oil or alcohol) that is at room temperature into the iSi whipper, followed by the infusion ingredient. Seal the iSi whipper and charge it with the gas cartridges. Swirl the iSi whipper for around 30 seconds, then leave it to rest for between 30 seconds and 2 minutes. The resting time will impact the intensity of the infusion: in some cases longer times will produce better outcomes; in others it will result in undesired flavors being infused, such as "bitterness" or "heat," so experimentation is necessary to achieve the desired outcome.

The next step is to gently release the gas from the iSi whipper. Once all the gas has been released, open the seal, allow the liquid (which will be bubbling) to settle, then pour the contents through a sieve, collecting the infused liquid in a bowl. The infused liquid can be served immediately or stored for later use.

### Tips

1. Use liquids that are at room temperature; cold liquids do not infuse as well.

2. Keep the nozzle of the iSi whipper pointing into a container as some liquid may spray out with the gas.

3. Using good-quality, fresh ingredients makes a big difference to the flavor of the resulting infusion.

4. Flavors will intensify by varying degrees based on how long the infused liquid is stored.

5. Try experimenting with different liquids, infusion ingredients and timings.

Hold the iSi whipper upright when releasing the gas.

# FIZZY GRAPES

### INGREDIENTS

10 oz (283 g) white grapes

1 cup (250 ml) white
grape juice

**Serves 6**

1. Place the grapes in the refrigerator overnight, and transfer them to the freezer 10 minutes before they are needed. They should be ice cold, although not frozen.

2. Wet the fruit and place it inside your iSi whipper.

3. Add the grape juice and seal the iSi whipper. Charge it with 2 carbon dioxide cartridges (iSi soda cartridges).

4. Refrigerate the iSi whipper for around 4 hours. The time required for the gas to dissolve into the fruit will vary with the type of fruit used, its size and wetness.

5. Remove the iSi whipper from the refrigerator and gently release the gas pressure, then unscrew the cover and pour out your carbonated grapes. The grapes will only stay carbonated for a short time, so serve them immediately. You can substitute all sorts of fruits, or even create a fizzy fruit cocktail.

### Serving suggestions:

- Fizzy grapes in Champagne (pictured opposite)

- Fizzy fruit salad

- Carbonated orange segments

# INSTANT LEMON-INFUSED OLIVE OIL

**INGREDIENTS**

2 oz (57 g) lemon zest
1 cup (250 ml) olive oil

**Makes 1 cup (250 ml)**

1. Put the lemon zest into your iSi whipper, then pour in the olive oil.

2. Seal the iSi whipper and charge it with 2 nitrous oxide gas cartridges (iSi cream chargers). Swirl the iSi whipper for around 30 seconds, then leave it to rest for 2 minutes.

3. Release the gas pressure from the iSi whipper, unscrew the cover then pour the infused olive oil out, straining it through a sieve to remove the zest.

### Serving suggestions:

- Vanilla-infused grapeseed oil
- Chili-infused groundnut oil

# INSTANT DILL-INFUSED VODKA

**INGREDIENTS USED**

2 oz (57 g) dill

1 cup (250 ml) vodka

**Serves 2**

1. Put the dill into your iSi whipper, then pour in the vodka.

2. Seal the iSi whipper and charge it with 2 nitrous oxide gas cartridges (iSi cream chargers). Swirl the iSi whipper for around 30 seconds, then leave it to rest for 2 minutes.

3. Release the gas pressure from the iSi whipper, unscrew the cover then pour the infused vodka into 2 cocktail glasses, straining it through a sieve to remove the dill.

## Serving suggestions:

- Cucumber and juniper berry-infused gin

- Coconut-infused rum

# TECHNIQUE 10: LIQUID NITROGEN

The conventional definition of cooking is considered to be primarily the process of preparing foods by heating. However, taking a more scientific perspective, cooking is about the physical and chemical reactions that alter the state of ingredients, making them edible. It can then be said that the removal of heat is an equally viable form of cooking. This may sound a little obscure, but think of a very common example: ice cream. So with this in mind, modernist chefs have introduced the use of liquid nitrogen into their kitchens.

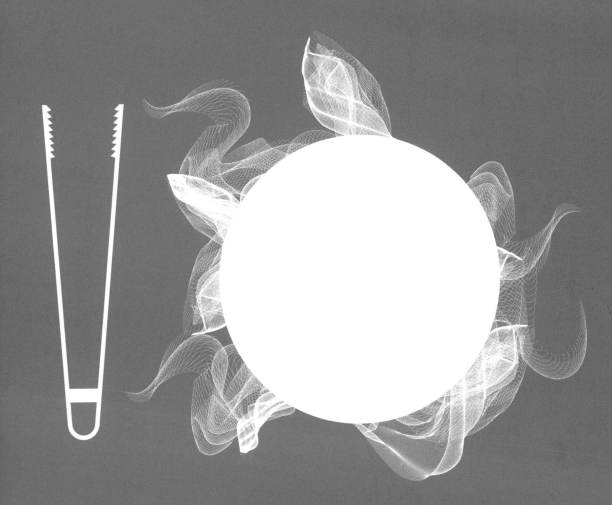

## What is Liquid Nitrogen?

Liquid nitrogen is a liquefied form of nitrogen. It is produced by liquefying air (air is comprised of around 78 percent nitrogen) and then separating the nitrogen by distillation. It is a very cold substance; at normal atmospheric pressure it has a boiling point of −321°F (−196°C), which makes it a cryogen — the term given to liquids that boil at a temperature below −256°F (−160°C).

## Original Uses

Due to its ability to maintain temperatures well below the freezing point of water, liquid nitrogen has been put to use in many ways, including preserving biological samples in laboratories and flash-freezing foods in the food manufacturing industry. Liquid nitrogen enables food manufacturers to freeze fresh foods while maintaining their texture, flavor and nutritional value, which would otherwise be degraded using regular freezing methods. The reason for this is that the cooling process is much faster using liquid nitrogen and therefore the ice crystals that form are far smaller than those that form when using regular methods.

Left: A delicious chilled ratatouillle is achieved using liquid nitrogen. Right: Michel Lentz chef of Les Fresques Royales restaurant, cooking herbs and high mountain pasture flowers with liquid nitrogen.

## Culinary Uses

The culinary potential of liquid nitrogen was first highlighted as far back as the late 19th century by Agnes Marshall, a cookbook writer who was nicknamed "The Queen of Ices." It was subsequently used in the production of ice cream by several culinary innovators throughout the 20th century. However, it wasn't until the early 2000s that liquid nitrogen really came to prominence. Chef Heston Blumenthal of The Fat Duck restaurant in the UK can, in many ways, be attributed with introducing the culinary world to the many applications of liquid nitrogen in the kitchen, his most popular liquid nitrogen creation being the "cryo-poached" green tea and lime mousse. Since then, chefs all over the world have been experimenting with liquid nitrogen. This has resulted in a whole host of different applications, including cryo-poaching (immersing foods — particularly liquids that form a frozen outer shell with a liquid center — in a liquid nitrogen bath), cryo-powders (foods immersed in liquid nitrogen then ground to a fine powder) and cryo-grating (foods immersed in liquid nitrogen then grated onto a dish).

The most common culinary use for liquid nitrogen is in making ice cream. This is actually a very simple process: the ice cream base is put in the metal bowl of an electric mixer with a flat paddle whisking attachment, the mixer is then switched on to a low–medium speed setting and the liquid nitrogen is added a little at a time. As liquid nitrogen has such rapid chilling properties it begins to freeze the ice cream base, instantaneously creating very small ice crystals, which results in a smooth and creamy texture. The ratio of liquid nitrogen to ice cream base is roughly 3:1 by weight. That means 12 cups (3 L) of liquid nitrogen will produce around 4 cups (1 L) of ice cream (this will vary as liquid nitrogen is quick to evaporate, and therefore up to 20 cups/5 L may be required).

You can also carry out the process using a metal mixing bowl and a whisk, which is how many restaurants make instant ice cream at the guest's table. This table-side display actually dates back to the 1970s at chef André Daguin's Hôtel de France in Auch, France. A cart would be rolled out into the dining room carrying a canister of liquid nitrogen and all the tools needed to make ice cream in front of the guest. Heston Blumenthal's Fat Duck restaurant creates its infamous egg and bacon ice cream in a similar table-side display.

It is important to note that liquid nitrogen is only used to chill foods very rapidly; it is not used as an ingredient and should not be ingested. Only once the liquid nitrogen has evaporated can the foods in which it has been used be consumed. Therefore foods that have been dipped in liquid nitrogen should be left to rest before serving, in a similar way to fried foods, which cannot be consumed straight out of the fryer without negative consequences.

Liquid nitrogen has many uses — using it to shuck oysters allows the shell to release far more easily than with traditional methods.

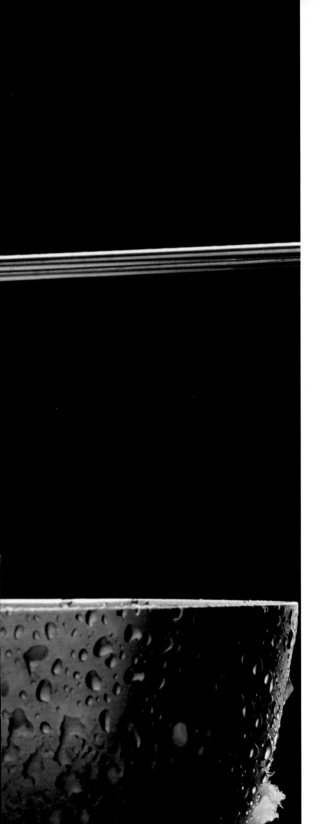

## Safety Issues

In many ways liquid nitrogen is no more dangerous than hot fryer oil, so it shouldn't be approached with too much trepidation. However, it is definitely not a substance to be toyed with, and direct contact with skin will cause burns.

Liquid nitrogen must be stored in special flasks or vessels (dewars), which are vacuum-insulated to prevent the transfer of heat and to reduce consumption through evaporation. While handling liquid nitrogen, it is recommended that you put on safety gloves and protective eyewear. Use stainless steel bowls and pans while cooking with liquid nitrogen as other materials do not handle the extremely cold temperature well: a glass bowl will shatter, just as it would if you poured 572°F (300°C) deep-frying fat into it.

The final safety issue concerns consumption. As noted on page 163, food should not be consumed until the liquid nitrogen has boiled off. The denser the food, the colder it will be and therefore the longer it will need to warm up.

When handling liquid nitrogen, always use stainless steel utensils and avoid materials that could shatter under cold temperatures.

# TECHNIQUE 11: THE ANTI-GRIDDLE

The Anti-Griddle is an innovative piece of kitchen equipment designed by PolyScience, an American-based company that has been developing precise temperature-controlling laboratory equipment since the early 1960s. PolyScience only became involved in producing kitchen equipment after they noticed that their immersion circulators were being purchased by restaurants, Alinea in Chicago among them. Since then PolyScience has worked with leading chefs, including Grant Achatz of Alinea, to develop a range of cutting-edge tools for forward-thinking chefs, resulting in products such as The Anti-Griddle and The Smoking Gun.

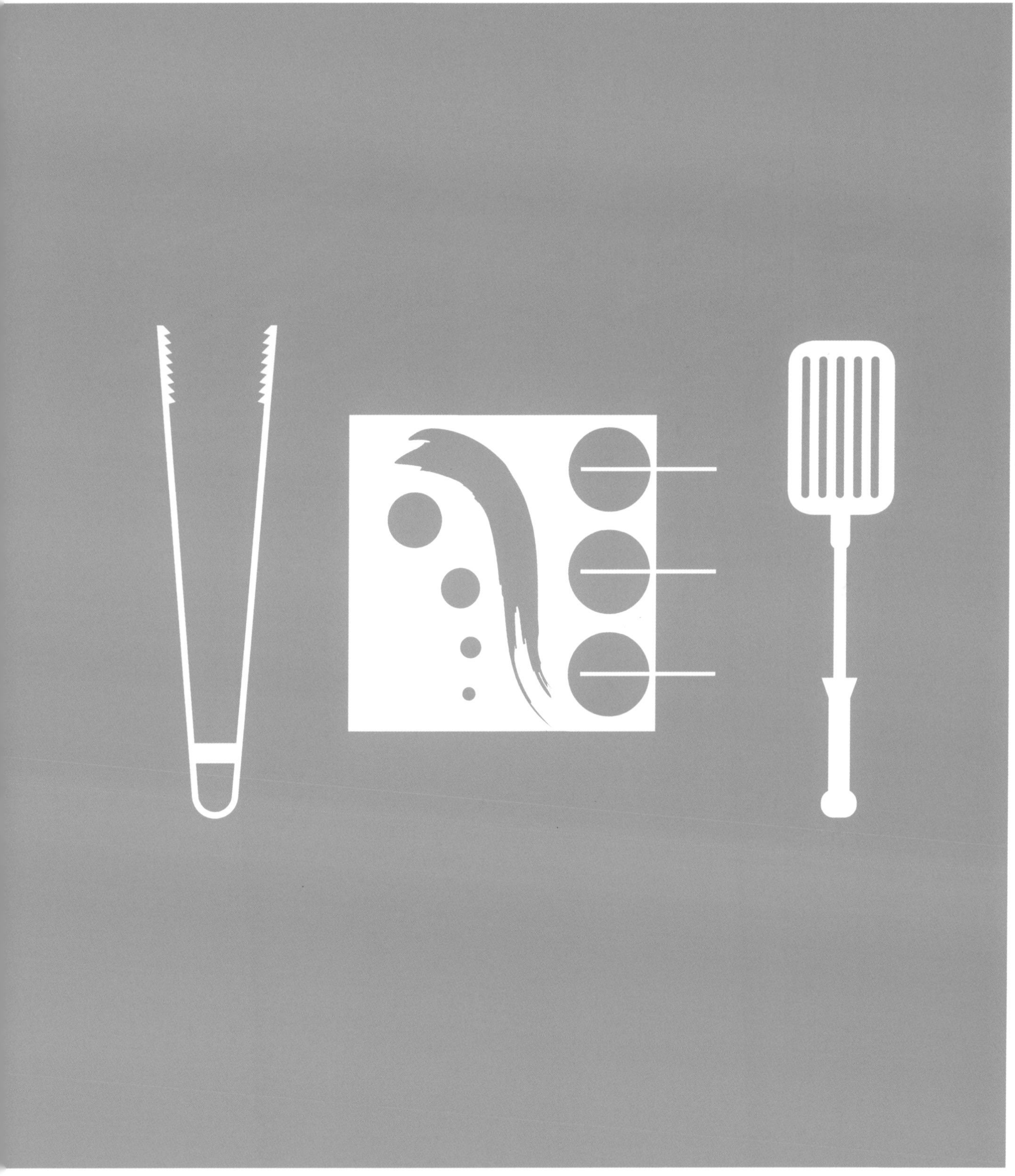

### What is The Anti-Griddle?

A regular griddle is a piece of cooking equipment consisting of a flat surface that heats up to around 536°F (280°C), using either gas or electricity. Food is cooked directly on the surface. A perfect example of its everyday use is in restaurants that serve hamburgers.

The Anti-Griddle, as its name suggests, performs quite the opposite task. Reaching a temperature of around −30°F (−34°C), it actually chills food rather than heats it. Although it lacks some of the theatrics of liquid nitrogen (see page 158), The Anti-Griddle does not have the associated risks, making it a much safer and more useful tool for the kitchen.

### How It Works

To reduce the likelihood of foods sticking to the surface of The Anti-Griddle, it is advisable to apply a light coating of oil prior to switching on the device. Some chefs also use parchment paper or plastic wrap to the same effect. Once switched on, The Anti-Griddle reaches its minimum temperature of −30°F (−34°C), which is non-adjustable, in between 10 and 15 minutes.

The Anti-Griddle is popular with a number of chefs including chef Pajo Bruich (above) and makes excellent frozen lollipops (left) and desserts.

As soon as it has reached its minimum temperature, The Anti-Griddle is ready for use and food can be placed directly onto its surface, where it will begin to chill instantaneously. The degree to which the food is chilled will depend on how long it is left on the surface of the device; this is where chefs get creative, chilling foods to varying degrees to produce a range of textures from semi-soft to frozen solid. Once it has reached the desired temperature the food is ready to serve immediately, or depending on its temperature, can be stored in the freezer for later consumption.

## Culinary Uses

Despite its single function, The Anti-Griddle can be used to create a wide range of innovative elements for both sweet and savory dishes. It can also be used to make novel canapés, frozen mousses, frozen vinaigrettes that melt when served, frozen lollipops created by pouring purée/mousse onto the surface of the device and placing a lollipop stick in its center, cakes or brownies coated in ice cream, and frozen desserts with cold liquid centers.

The Anti-Griddle allows chefs to make show-stopping food items like this strawberry cube with frozen pepper brittle.

# TECHNIQUE 12: CENTRIFUGE

Certain techniques and equipment discussed in this book are not readily accessible to the home cook; centrifuge most definitely falls into this category. In fact, the few restaurants that do own a centrifuge are employing equipment that was intended for use by scientists in laboratories, not by chefs in kitchens. Centrifuges have only recently found their way into kitchens.

The principles upon which centrifuges operate are the same as those at work in much more common household equipment, including washers and dryers, centrifugal juicers and salad spinners.

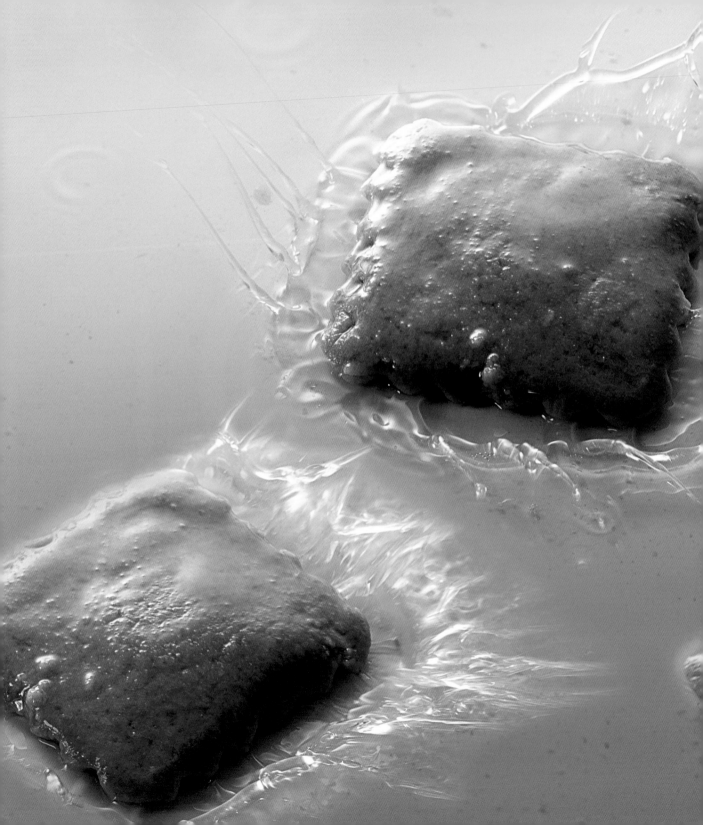

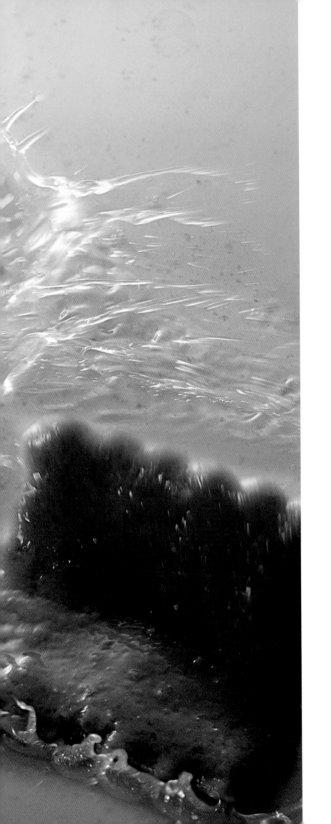

## What Is a Centrifuge?

A centrifuge separates mixtures based on their density (their mass per unit volume). Liquids or solids that are less dense will float on those that are more dense. In practical terms, it is the difference in density that causes eggs to sink and apples to float in water; differences in density also explain why fats rise in a stock pot and bones fall to the bottom.

A very simple experiment that demonstrates differences in densities is to take a glass and pour in oil, vinegar and rock salt. Their relative densities will cause them to separate: the oil will float to the top, the rock salt will sink to the bottom, and the vinegar will remain in the middle.

A centrifuge is capable of creating this type of separation in almost all mixtures.

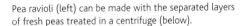

Pea ravioli (left) can be made with the separated layers of fresh peas treated in a centrifuge (below).

## How It Works

Mixtures are put into containers that are then sealed and placed into the centrifuge. The centrifuge spins these containers at extremely high speeds, exerting forces upon the mixtures that can reach hundreds of thousands of times the strength of gravity. These forces cause mixtures to separate into their component parts based on density.

There are three main types of centrifuge: those with fixed angles, which keep the sample containers at a constant tilt; those with hinges that hold the sample containers and allow them to swing outward during the spinning process; and tubular centrifuges, which don't use sample containers and are employed when large volumes are required.

## Culinary Uses

Much like rotary evaporators, they are not a common sight in restaurant kitchens. There are of course very simple centrifuges on the market in the form of centrifugal juicers, which separate juices from their pulp.

To date, the potential culinary applications of a centrifuge have been best explored by the team behind the *Modernist Cuisine* books. Their culinary endeavors introduced the world to pea butter, which is produced by puréeing frozen peas then placing the purée in a centrifuge for 1 hour at 27,500g; the result is three separated layers consisting of pea solids (at the bottom), pea fat (in the center) and pea water (at the top).

Each separated layer opens doors to potential new elements for a dish, yet it is pea butter that really steals the show due to its complete uniqueness.

# TECHNIQUE 13: ROTARY EVAPORATOR

A rotary evaporator, commonly known as a "rotovap," is an apparatus that, until recently, was only used in chemical laboratories. Its primary function is the separation of a mixture into its components based on their respective volatilities — a process called "distillation." However, this piece of equipment adds an additional dimension to the regular process of distillation by carrying it out under vacuum. Distillation under vacuum lowers the boiling point of a mixture to room temperature. Processing distillations at low temperatures results in valuable flavor compounds being preserved much more effectively than is the case with traditional methods, in which many of the more delicate flavor and aroma compounds are lost due to the high temperatures required.

Distillation separates a liquid's volatile components, such as aroma, alcohol, water and small flavor molecules, from its non-volatile components, such as sugar, acid, bitterness, sourness, heat and color. This is achieved through evaporation (turning a liquid into a gas) and condensation (turning a gas back into a liquid).

Traditional distillation processes have been used for centuries — ancient civilizations are known to have distilled fermented beverages to produce drinks with increased alcohol contents — and are performed at temperatures of around 170°F–200°F (77°C–93°C). It is important to note that, at these temperatures, the liquid being distilled is altered by the heat, which affects its flavor molecules.

### What Is a Rotary Evaporator?

The distillation process, when it is carried out by a rotary evaporator, can be called "vacuum distillation" or "cold distillation." The device distills at much lower temperatures than those used by traditional distillation methods as it performs the process under vacuum. The vacuum reduces the atmospheric pressure, lowering the boiling point and allowing volatile components to evaporate at far lower temperatures, thus preserving their original characteristics. Simply put, a rotary evaporator allows liquids to vaporize at room temperature, meaning they are not cooked and therefore the quality of the flavor molecules is better preserved.

Innovative chefs use this vacuum distillation process to extract and capture delicate flavor components that would otherwise be altered or destroyed by the higher temperatures of the regular distillation process.

### How It Works

To understand how a rotary evaporator works it is good to have an idea of the key components from which it is assembled. The following is a list of the main parts and the functions they perform.

1. A motorized unit rotates the evaporation flask that contains the mixture to be distilled.

2. A water-bath provides a gentle source of heat in which the evaporation flask is partly submerged.

3. A vacuum system lowers the boiling point of the mixture in the evaporation flask.

4. A condensing coil cools the vapor from the evaporation flask back into a liquid, which then trickles down the coil.

5. A receiving flask catches the distilled liquid.

Two elements in particular distinguish the rotary evaporator from traditional distillation equipment. First there is the vacuum, which as mentioned previously, allows for lower boiling points; the second is the rotation of the evaporation flask in a temperature-controlled water-bath. The second component works to increase the surface area of the mixture being distilled while gently heating it; this speeds up the process and ensures an even rate of evaporation.

The rate of distillation is affected by the temperature of the water-bath (although this will not raise the mixture's temperature to above its boiling point), the pressure of the vacuum (this directly affects the boiling point), the size and rotation speed of the evaporation flask and the size and power of the system's condenser.

### Culinary Uses

The rotary evaporator was first brought to chefs' attention by chef Joan Roca of El Celler de Can Roca in Spain during a culinary conference in 2005, when he demonstrated its potential culinary uses. He had been using it to create a dish in which he served an oyster in a clear jelly that is flavored with the distilled aroma of forest soil.

Since then chefs have used this vacuum distillation process to explore ways of separating flavors — for example it can draw off the aromatics of a chili pepper while leaving behind capsaicin, which gives peppers their heat. It has also been used to concentrate flavors and extract aromas by separating different flavor molecules, for example, to get the purest and freshest flavor from an orange by removing the water from the fruit.

Chef Grant Achatz of Alinea in Chicago extracts herbal aromas from lemon grass, basil and chilis. In the case of

chili, during this process capsaicin is left behind (eliminating the heat), with only the pure essence being captured.

Dave Arnold, Director of Culinary Technology at the French Culinary Institute in New York, highlighted the fact that alcohol-based solutions produce fresher and more vibrant distillations than water-based solutions. He has developed recipes for spirits such as horseradish, habaneros and chocolate, which are full of aroma yet carry none of the pungency, heat or bitterness related to their respective ingredients. He has also developed a Scotch flavored with peanuts; and a deconstructed port, which he serves with Stilton cheese and an oak-flavored ice cream that is made

by separating the oak notes from an aged Scotch and then freezing this liquid using liquid nitrogen — the result is said to carry all the vanilla, spice and maple notes of the wood, as well as an inescapable flavor of briny lumber.

As a final point, it is important to be aware that, although owning a rotary evaporator is perfectly legal, and distilling water-based mixtures is fine, the distillation of alcohol without a license is illegal in some countries.

Alcohol-based solutions work very well for distillation, creating fresh new liquors such as horseradish and chocolate.

# TECHNIQUE 14: ULTRA-SONIC HOMOGENIZER

In the modern chef's kitchen, homogenizing means that a mixture is either mixed, blended, emulsified, dispersed or stirred until it has the same composition throughout — that is, it is homogenous. Most kitchens contain various tools that can be used to homogenize a mixture, including jug blenders, hand-held immersion blenders, food processors and even a simple whisk.

It is far less common to find an ultra-sonic homogenizer in a kitchen. Innovative chefs have discovered that this high-tech piece of laboratory equipment can be put to good culinary use for extracting and infusing flavors, for homogenizing and emulsifying liquids, as well as for de-gassing wine and giving the effect of barrel-aging in alcohol.

## What Is an Ultra-Sonic Homogenizer?

There are various types of high-tech homogenizers, including high-pressure homogenizers, rotor stator homogenizers and blade homogenizers, all of which operate using different mechanical actions. However, for the purpose of this chapter, ultra-sonic homogenizers are the focus as the principles on which they work are just that bit cooler.

Ultra-sonic homogenizers are typically used in laboratories to disrupt things like bacteria, spores and soil samples. Unlike other homogenizing tools, an ultra-sonic homogenizer uses soundwaves rather than mechanical action to reduce particles in a liquid so that they become uniformly small and evenly distributed (that is, homogenous).

An ultra-sonic homogenizer emulsifies liquids very easily, shown by these different stages of water mixed with chili oil.

## How It Works

Ultra-sonic homogenizers have three main components: an electric generator that creates a signal; a transducer that transforms the signal into mechanical energy; and a probe that amplifies the vibrations all the way down its length.

As the vibrations work their way down the probe the intense sonic pressure waves cause alternating high- and low-pressure cycles within liquids. During the low-pressure cycles, high-intensity vacuum micro-bubbles form in the liquid. The bubbles grow and coalesce, eventually imploding violently and generating shockwaves. This process is called "cavitation." The forces at work have enough energy to break up liquids into smaller and smaller particles and disrupt cell walls.

It's the cavitation phenomenon that causes the dispersion of fat into tiny droplets within an emulsion, keeping it stable for days without the use of emulsifiers or stabilizers. It is also cavitation that releases flavor molecules from ingredients by disrupting their cell walls and dispersing them into a liquid.

## Culinary Uses

An ultra-sonic homogenizer generates little heat. This means that the natural colors, nutritional values, aromas and other flavor characteristics of food are hardly altered by the process. Most processes can be completed in a matter of minutes (for example, making vinaigrette). However, this high-end piece of equipment also speeds up results that could otherwise take years to achieve; to this end, it has been used to create rapidly aged alcoholic drinks by infusing them with woodchips. It has also been used to de-gas and homogenize wine (altering its mouth feel), and to intensify stocks and fruit or vegetable pulp for sauces (by disrupting cells).

A close-up of the ultra-sonic homogenizer's tip shows how it creates an instant cloud in the liquid.

# TECHNIQUE 15: FERMENTATION

Fermentation is an age-old preservation process, which, as with culinary smoking (see page 148), has recently undergone a revival among some of the world's leading modernist chefs.

The most common fermented products are sauerkraut and other pickled foods. You are probably familiar with a greater number of fermented foods than you think. When you have toast for breakfast, or any form of bread, you are eating a product that has undergone fermentation; the same goes for cheese, cured meats and yogurt. Alcoholic beverages such as wine, cider and beer are all fermented, as are the non-alcoholic beverages coffee and tea. Popular fermented Asian condiments and dishes, such as fish sauce, soy sauce, kimchi and miso, are also becoming more common in the Western kitchen.

Some fermented foods are much more widely appreciated and enjoyed than others. Along with some of the foods mentioned above, miso soup and Indian dosai have a wide fan-base; on the other hand, Japanese nato (fermented beans), Nepalese gundruk (a fermented green vegetable) and Sudanese fermented cow's milk are considered more of an acquired taste.

As we live in an age of pasteurization, the notion of letting your food spoil may seem counterintuitive. However, the process of fermentation brings various nutritional and flavor-enhancing benefits, not to mention endless new flavors developed by some of the world's leading chefs.

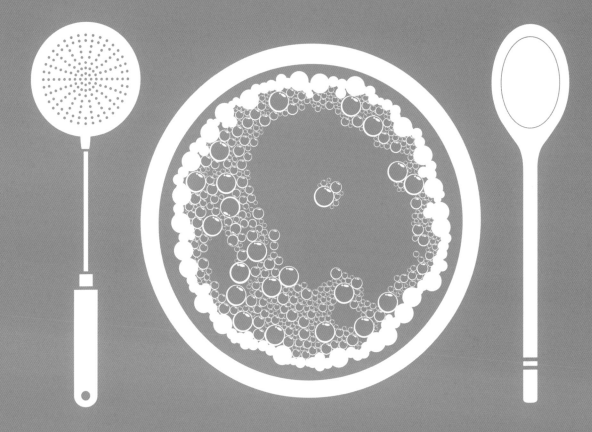

## History of Fermentation

The origins of fermentation as a food-processing technique are ancient. Cave drawings dating back 12,000 years show men obtaining honey from hives to make mead (a form of wine made from honey). Traditionally, fermentation was a form of preservation and a way of storing foods while retaining their nutrients. Many early fermented vegetables, including cabbage (made into sauerkraut), simply had salt added to them; the lactic acid this produced prevented putrefaction and preserved the nutritional value, keeping people fed through the winter.

Captain James Cook, the 18th-century English explorer, was recognized by the Royal Society for conquering scurvy, a disease caused by vitamin C deficiency that had plagued sailors of that era. He reduced occurrences of the disease by feeding his crew sauerkraut for 27 months during their second tour around the world.

By the 19th century, French chemist Louis Pasteur — the first zymologist (someone skilled in the area of applied science related to fermentation) — connected yeast to fermentation. Pasteur originally defined fermentation as "respiration without air."

In the early 20th century Nobel Prize winner Dr. Élie Metchnikoff was one of the first scientists to recognize the nutritional benefits of eating fermented foods. His research focused on the Bulgarians and he attributed their superior health and longevity to their daily intake of yogurt.

We now know that fermentation increases the amounts of some vitamins in foods, and that fermented products are a great source of amino acids, vitamins and minerals. Fermented milk, for instance, is a fantastic source of

Bacterial fermentation is used to preserve vegetables in a pickle. This process enhances their flavor as well as introducing nutritious cultures to the human digestive system.

energetic B vitamins, while fermented vegetable dishes, like kimchi (Korean fermented cabbage) supply vitamins C and A. Search for probiotics on the internet and you will come up with a host of reasons why "good bacteria" are beneficial for you.

## The Science Behind Fermentation

Fermented foods are transformed by the introduction of good bacteria or fungi. In food processing, fermentation usually refers to the conversion of carbohydrates to alcohols and carbon dioxide, or organic acids, using yeasts, bacteria or a combination of the two, under anaerobic conditions (where no oxygen is present). Fermentation is thus underpinned by an acidic environment in which few harmful organisms survive.

Ethanol fermentation, also known as alcoholic fermentation, is carried out using yeasts. These can be found everywhere: in your garden, on your hands, in the air and on the surface of some fruits. While they are members of the fungi family and are living creatures, they can survive even if there is no oxygen and will continue to break down sugars. This type of fermentation occurs in the production of alcoholic beverages and in the rising of bread dough. It is a biological process in which the yeast uses alcoholic fermentation to break down sugars, converting them into cellular energy, and thereby producing ethanol and carbon dioxide as metabolic waste products. In summary, carbohydrate/sugar + yeast + time = alcohol + $CO_2$.

Ethanol (pure alcohol) gives beer, wine and spirits their alcoholic content. The alcohol also provides flavor in bread, with the carbon dioxide gas forming bubbles or pockets of air that lift the dough and eventually diffuse out of the bread while it is baking, making it lighter. When the

Chef René Redzepi of Noma is renowned for his experimentation with fermentation, and he even posts instruction clips online to help budding molecular gastronomists.

yeasts have done their work they are killed off. Baking bread kills the yeast that has produced the carbon dioxide that helped the bread to rise. In producing alcohol in a closed environment, the alcohol eventually kills the yeast.

Bacterial fermentation is a process by which beneficial bacteria convert complex or simple sugars in dairy products, vegetables or fruit to lactic acid, or in some cases, acetic acid. Bacteria are either single or multi-cell organisms that are found almost everywhere in nature, often contributing to food spoilage. However, as mentioned earlier, beneficial bacteria also exist.

This type of fermentation is nearly always used as a preservative agent for vegetables. For example, cabbages are preserved to make sauerkraut or Korean kimchi; pickles are preserved to make Chinese hum choi or Nepalese gundruk. As well as enhancing flavors and adding nutritive value to food, lactic acid and living lactobacillus cultures are beneficial to the human digestive system. Foods loaded with these elements are considered medicinal by traditional medical practitioners, a view supported by scientific research. The sour taste that we recognize and look for in many foods such as buttermilk, yogurt, sauerkraut, pickles, sourdough bread and even olives, results from the acids produced by fermentation. As the acidity level increases, harmful bacteria are killed off, making food safe for storage and subsequent consumption.

In mold fermentation, molds can act as preservers or spoilers depending on the type and how they are treated. The aspergillus mold is often associated with food spoilage, though it is heavily used in Asian cuisines for fermented foods. Aspergillus oryzae, also known as koji, has been used for hundreds of years in the production of soy sauce, miso and sake. In the koji process, fungal enzymes perform the same function as the malting enzymes used in beer fermentations. The koji molds release amylases that break down rice starch, which in turn can be fermented to make rice wine. Koji molds are also effective in a variety of legume fermentations, of which miso and soy sauce are the best known.

Molds from the genus *Penicillium* are associated with the ripening and flavoring of cheeses. *Penicillium camemberti* and *Penicillium roqueforti* are the molds on Camembert, Brie, Roquefort and many other cheeses. *Penicillium nalgiovense* is used to improve the taste of sausages and hams, and to prevent colonization by other molds and bacteria.

## Getting Started at Home

Before discussing home fermentation in detail, it is important to highlight a few important points.

Fermentation is only good for you if it occurs outside your body, meaning that if you ingest foods that provide an abundance of sugar and growth media for bacteria, they will ferment those foods inside you. An overgrowth of fermentative bacteria in your body can cause all kinds of medical problems. Though such cases are rare, fermented foods can be overtaken by mold or become spoiled, so take care not to eat them if this occurs.

## Ethanol Fermentation

To make wine, first press grapes to extract their juice (which contains naturally occurring sugars), then transfer the juice to a sterilized container, such as a barrel. Next add the bacteria (yeast), this will interact with the sugars, eventually converting them into ethanol and $CO_2$ (and in this case, wine). Fermentation allows us to make wine, cider and similar alcoholic beverages up to an ABV (alcohol by volume) of around 15 percent before a number of natural factors stop the process. If we want something a bit stronger, distillation plays a role. This is a simplified method — modern wine production has science and method behind it. If you want to ferment your own alcohol, there are many brewing kits available online that will provide you with all the tools you will need.

## Lactic Acid Fermentation

All kinds of fruits and vegetables can be preserved using this method, most notably cucumbers, cabbage, carrots, green beans, pearl onions, radishes, tomatoes, turnips, zucchini, eggplant and snow peas. The variety of fruits is equally diverse: plums, peaches, pears, apples, mangoes, papayas, lemons, raisins, oranges, apricots, berries and more.

This method of fermentation couldn't be easier: wash and cut, chop or shred your chosen fruits or vegetables. Combine them with herbs or spices, and sea salt, and press them down tightly into an airtight container (such as a mason jar), to partially release their juices. Keep the tightly sealed container at room temperature for 2–3 days to allow the good bacteria to proliferate. The salt keeps the bacteria from putrefying until enough lactic acid is created, thus preserving the food for months. At this point, the fermented fruits or vegetables can be stored in the refrigerator.

## Fermentation and Umami

Along with its many health and nutrition-boosting benefits, fermentation can also increase the umami in foods, especially in soy sauce, cheese and cured meats. Umami-rich ingredients from Asia may appear to be an unrelated group of food items: wine, kimchee, pickled and preserved vegetables, mushrooms, rice and vinegar. Yet all these foods involve fungi or bacteria in some shape or form.

As we have already established, yeast metabolizes sugar through fermentation, which produces alcohol. When you add yeast (in a controlled environment) to a fruit juice or grain cooked in water, the result is an alcoholic beverage. It is during the aging process (after the primary fermentation is complete) that umami enters the equation. Asian rice wines like Huangjiu, mirin and sake are rounded, full-bodied and crisp, with a rich, sweet finish. As with European fortified wines, like sherry and Madeira, these Asian rice wines gain even more character and flavor when aged; the amount of umami flavor also increases.

According to the Nordic Food Lab, salt-rich fermentations can be used to create a high level of umami. Such fermentations are often used to create food products rich both in acid and in umami, due to the enzymatic activity on proteins (especially in legumes, meat and fish). This explains the number of umami-rich Asian sauces that are becoming a staple part of the Western pantry.

## Fermentation in the Modern Kitchen

All this explains why this age-old food-preservation technique is undergoing a revival by the world's leading chefs. Fermented foods are healthy and nutritious and packed with umami. But, more importantly, fermentation offers chefs a new way of improving, transforming, and in some cases augmenting, the flavors of foods. As with other recent culinary trends (including molecular cooking and the farm-to-table movement), fermentation is fresh territory for creative expression.

Chef René Redzepi, of the Noma restaurant in Copenhagen, Denmark, and gastronomic entrepreneur Claus Meyer established the Nordic Food Lab, led by the head of culinary research, Ben Reade. Here, research into fermentation has led to culinary innovations, including "fermented grasshoppers," "lacto-fermented plums" and a "yeast petit four."

"It has nothing to do with shock value or trying to be novel in that sense ... It's a search for flavors," explains René Redzepi. Meanwhile, chef David Chang's Momofuku research lab in New York, USA, which is headed by Dan Felder (who works with Harvard University microbiologists), has focused on concocting new flavors from microbes and mold, one of which is "pistachio miso."

"In a world where flavors are becoming increasingly redundant and the same, it's refreshing to taste something that's bright and new, even though it's rotten and old," says David Chang.

# HYDROCOLLOIDS

This book contains two chapters which focus on gels (see pages 102–131), all of which are classified as hydrocolloids. Other than the six gelling agents referred to in these chapters, there are a whole host of others which have various properties and are useful either on their own or in a wide range of combinations.

To fully grasp how gelling agents work and the underlying principles of their use, this chapter will define all the associated terms that will help you gain a better understanding of gels as well as their characteristics and potential uses.

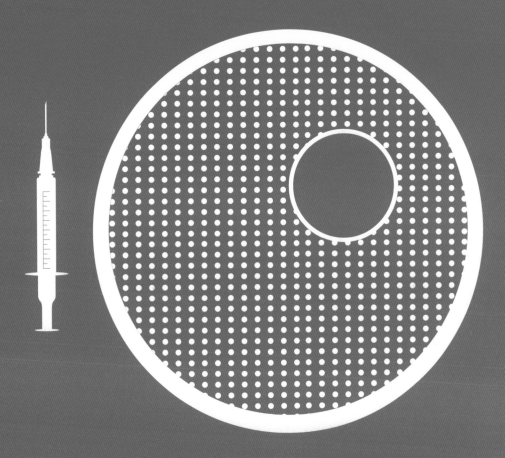

## What is a Hydrocolloid?

Hydrocolloids are systems in which particles are dispersed in water, and depending on the quantity of water, the results will be either a gel (like a regular jelly) or a sol (which is a suspension of very small particles in liquid, for example milk).

A colloid is a substance that is microscopically dispersed evenly throughout another substance. Colloidal systems can be made up of solids, liquids or gases and are comprised of two separate phases: the dispersed phase and the continuous phase. To help put all this into context, here are a few examples of colloidal systems and their comprising phases: whipped cream (liquid is the continuous phase and gas is the dispersed phase), milk (both phases are liquid) and smoke (gas is the continuous phase and solids are the dispersed phase).

Hydrocolloids are colloidal systems in which the colloid particles are dispersed in water (so the continuous phase is always liquid). Put into very simple terms: hydrocolloids (also referred to as gels) are substances that can thicken solutions and form gels as well as forming stable foams, emulsions and dispersions.

Each type of hydrocolloid has different properties related to its physical structure, which is determined by the sugars it is consisted of, and will react differently to acidity, temperature and mechanical action. So when using hydrocolloids, much of your decision on which one to use will depend on the type of gel or sol you wish to create, the ingredients you are using and the temperature at which you want to serve it. It is also important to note that other than gelatin (which is a protein), all hydrocolloids are polysaccharides or complex sugars. It is because of this

These Japanese gelatin candies are made using agar-agar to create a jelly-like texture.

that when dispersed in water, the water is attracted to and gathers around the sugar. This causes layers of water with restricted movement to be formed, and by controlling the water a gel or sol is created.

## Where do Hydrocolloids Come From?

Contrary to popular belief, gelling agents are not the big bad wolf they are made out to be. In fact many hydrocolloids are derived from natural sources, including seaweed, seeds, roots, tree sap and fruit. And although many of these "additives" may sound new or foreign to you, in some cases they have been in use for thousands of years by different cultures around the world.

Take agar agar, which is derived from seaweed; this is relatively new to the pantry of any Western kitchen, however the Japanese have been using it for several centuries as a gelling agent in desserts. Only recently has the Western world come to realize its potential as a vegetarian alternative to the more commonly used gelatin (which is traditionally derived from animal bones). Carrageenan is another example. As with agar agar it is derived from seaweed and has been used by the Irish for hundreds of years as a gelling agent. You also have gum arabic (derived from tree sap), locust bean gum (derived from seeds) and pectin (which occurs naturally in fruits and is the traditional gelling agent used for making jam).

Then you have more modern gelling agents like xanthan gum, which is a natural product formed by the fermentation of glucose, sucrose or lactose by the *Xanthomonas campestris* bacterium. Gellan gum is another example. Finally you have gelling agents which are still safe to consume, however they are produced by the modification of ingredients to create compounds not found in nature, such as methyl cellulose.

## Characteristics of Gels

When gels are referred to in this book you may come across terms which are new to you. Most of these will be related to the characteristics of gels. The following is a breakdown.

- **Clarity:** Some gelling agents create gels which have a very clear and transparent appearance; other agents create gels with a more hazy appearance.

- **Flavor release:** Related to how well the gels carry the flavor of the ingredient to which they are added. Some do this very well while others tend to lock up the flavors, inhibiting the taste of the main flavor when consumed. The degree with which hydrocolloid solutions mix with saliva, determined by their degree of chain entanglement, determines flavor perception.

- **Thermo-reversible:** The gel will melt when heated to a high enough temperature. Methyl cellulose is an exception as it forms gels when heated and melts as it cools.

- **Thermo-irreversible:** The gel will not melt when heated.

- **Syneresis:** This is when liquid leaks out of the gel over time; it is not the same as melting. This may take longer in some gels than others: harder gels tend to experience greater syneresis than soft ones, and generally most gels that are frozen will leak when thawed.

- **Freeze–thaw stability:** Any gel which can be frozen and thawed without degrading its structure is considered freeze–thaw stable. Many gels are structurally compromised by freezing (causing syneresis and textural changes) and are considered to have poor freeze–thaw stability.

- **Shearing:** The force created by stirring or whisking; in this context it is the gels' ability to re-form after being stirred or whisked. Some gels will break under shear, which means the gel is broken down and will no longer re-form after being subjected to such mechanical force. Gels which do re-form are termed shear reversible.

- **Shear thinning:** Most gels tend to get thinner as they are sheared (stirred or whisked).

- **Yield point:** Some gels appear as gels when still and liquefy instantly under shear. Xanthan gum is a great example, as it can appear as a gel yet with sufficient force it will flow in a liquid-like manner.

## Using Hydrocolloids

As mentioned earlier in this chapter, it is important to understand more about each of the gelling agents you wish to use in order to make sure you are using the right agent for the job and that the method in which you use it is suitable to the agent. You should take the following considerations into account.

*Temperature:* When using gels, temperature is a very important factor in creating them, holding them and presenting them. Some gels require hydration in cold solutions, others in hot solutions and some can be hydrated in either hot or cold solutions. Most gels will have a setting temperature that is lower than their melting temperature, some gels can be melted down and will gel again when cooled, others won't. There are gels such as agar agar-based gels which can be held at room temperature and even heated up to a certain point, and others like gelatin which must be kept in the refrigerator until you are ready to serve them.

*pH:* Most gelling agents are pH sensitive, so their effectiveness will vary depending on the pH of the solution to which they are added. The basic spherification technique will not work as effectively, if at all, when the sodium alginate is added to a solution which is highly acidic. The acidity of a solution can be neutralized using sodium citrate, however this can also impact the flavor of the solution.

*Combinations:* Not all gelling agents work in the same way when used in combination with other agents as their characteristics can be altered. For example, when used separately xanthan gum and locust bean gum are thickeners rather than gelling agents, however when mixed they form a gel. This effect can be advantageous as it can allow you to create gels with unique characteristics.

*Hydration:* This step is vital to the formation of proper gels, and can cause a recipe to either work or fail. Gelling agents must be hydrated and dissolved into a solution in order to be effective; if not they will form lumps that won't dissolve, similar to the lumps of corn starch in gravy. To avoid lumps, gelling agents must be dispersed properly before they can dissolve. The dispersion process causes hydrocolloid particles to be forced as far apart from each other as possible before they begin to absorb water (hydrate) and swell. There are two methods of dispersion: the first is to blend the mix using high shear, with either a hand-held immersion blender or a regular blender (if using a regular blender, sprinkle the gelling agent into the center of the vortex created as it will aid dispersion). The second is to disperse the hydrocolloid in a solution in which it will not dissolve then change the conditions to allow it to dissolve. An everyday example of this is the method you use to mix corn starch into a gravy: first you mix it into cold water (in which it will not dissolve) then you stir this into the gravy, which creates a smooth, thickened result.

Each gelling agent has its own hydration procedures, but in general hydrocolloids are most suited to hydration in pure (pH neutral) water. Sugar, starch, alcohol or salt can obstruct the hydration process as they compete with the hydrocolloid for water.

*Quantities and measurements:* Gelling agents are usually measured as a percentage of the overall mass of the solution, so four cups (1 L) of a 1 percent xanthan solution should consist of 3.96 cups (937 ml) of water and 0.04 cups (9 ml) of xanthan, however in practical terms we tend to measure a 1 percent solution by adding 0.04 cups (9 ml) of xanthan to four cups (1 L) of water. The small variation will not cause a huge disruption to the process, however it is important to have an accurate scale on hand which can measure to 0.003 fluid ounces (0.1 ml) and even better if it can measure to 0.0003 fluid ounces (0.01 ml).

*Calcium and potassium:* Some gelling agents instantly form gels which are not properly hydrated in the presence of calcium and potassium; this is called pre-gelation. In the spherification process, for example, sodium alginate will immediately begin to react if added to yogurt (due to its high calcium content) and therefore the mixture will not create proper yogurt spheres, hence the reverse spherification process is used for high calcium ingredients. Be aware of the amount of calcium in tap water as this can affect your results.

Sequestrants can be added to solutions in order to reduce the chances of pre-gelation. Sequestrants are food additives which improve the quality and stability of food products, the most common types being sodium citrate, calcium lactate and calcium gluconate.

### Commonly Used Hydrocolloids

Agar agar, carrageenan, corn starch, gelatin, gellan, guar gum, gum arabic, locust bean gum, maltodextrin, methyl cellulose, pectin, sodium alginate, xanthan.

# UMAMI

To many people the term "umami" is completely foreign. If you too are not sure what to expect from this chapter don't panic — just keep reading!

Umami is a Japanese word and its direct translation is "delicious taste" or "pleasant savory taste." It is now recognized as our fifth taste along with sweet, salty, sour and bitter. If you are now wondering what umami tastes like, and if you have ever tasted it, let's put it this way: most people first encounter umami in breast milk (which contains high levels of umami).

At its simplest, umami is a savory taste which is most commonly associated with cured meats, certain types of seafood (especially anchovies), mushrooms, seaweed, tomatoes (even ketchup), cheese (especially Parmesan), soy sauce and British meat extracts such as Bovril and yeast extracts like Marmite. Most people find it hard to identify umami at first as they are not attuned to it and do not look out for it when tasting foods. Umami is far more subtle than the other four tastes and is known for blending well with them; in some cases it enhances them — particularly sweetness and saltiness — and creates more rounded and full-flavored dishes.

## The History of Umami

Over the last decade umami has increased in popularity. This is in part due to the rise in popularity of Japanese food (mainly sushi, tempura and teriyaki) and in part because some of the world's most media-friendly chefs, including Ferran Adrià and Heston Blumenthal (both of whom have written forewords to books on the subject), have promoted its importance in the overall flavor of dishes.

Although umami has only recently been recognized as an independent flavor, it has existed in our food throughout history. An ingredient called garum — a fermented fish sauce rich in glutamate — was used in the cuisines of ancient Greece, Rome and Byzantium. The Japanese have eaten umami-rich foods for centuries with dashi — a seaweed and bonito stock — considered the heart of Japanese cuisine.

Despite umami being part of international cuisine for so long, it wasn't until 1908 that it was identified. Professor Kikunae Ikeda of Tokyo Imperial University discovered a taste in dashi that could not be accounted for using the existing four tastes. As part of his research he identified brown crystals which remained after dashi had been evaporated as glutamic acid. When he tasted these crystals he detected a flavor existent in many foods. After naming his discovery "umami" he then patented the mass production of a crystalline salt of glutamic acid — monosodium glutamate or MSG. Following this, other sources of umami were discovered: in 1913 Shintaro Kodama found that it was the chemical (inosinate) released from katsuobushi (dried, fermented and smoked skipjack tuna) (see dashi table) that elevated the umami taste in dashi. Then, in 1957, Akira Kininaka figured out that guanylate, a compound found in dried shiitake mushrooms, also contributed an umami flavor. Initially, scientists in the West thought that only the Japanese could detect umami and did not share the belief that umami was a basic taste. But in 2000 the discovery of an umami taste receptor in human taste buds (dubbed taste-mGluR4) secured umami the position of the fifth taste.

## Dashi

Dashi has been used in Japanese cooking for several hundred years, it is considered the heart of Japanese cooking and is used as the base for many soups and sauces in the same way that meat stocks such as chicken, beef or veal are regarded as the foundations of French cuisine.

However, there are major differences between Western stocks and dashi; first of all the flavor in dashi is much more subtle and merely captures the essence of its ingredients while most Western stocks present quite strong flavors and are judged on whether they have extracted the maximum amount of flavor from their ingredients. Dashi is prized not for the prominence of its own flavor, but for the way in which it enhances and harmonizes the flavors of other ingredients. The second difference relates to the preparation; while Western stocks are prepared by simmering meat and vegetables in water over a long period of time, dashi uses ingredients which are matured for long periods, then soaked in water and briefly heated to around 140°F–149°F (60°C–65°C) to extract their flavor.

There are several varieties of dashi, each one distinguished by the combination of ingredients used. The one ingredient common to all dashi is kombu, a type of seaweed known as kelp in English. Kombu is most commonly harvested in July through September from the waters off Hokkaido in

Umami is a savory taste commonly associated with cured Charcuterie meats. The meats pictured right were prepared by Rob Ruban, Executive Chef of Crossbar in New York.

northern Japan. Once brought to shore it is laid out to dry in the sun before being taken indoors where the fronds are shaped. Some kombu undergoes further treatment. The kombu is then stored in a cellar for up to ten years (similar to the way in which wine is stored) where the maturation process known as kuragakoi takes place. This process aims to increase the levels of umami in the kombu.

## Different Types of Dashi

| | |
|---|---|
| Ichiban dashi | The most prized of all the dashi, it is made from kombu and katsubushi (dried bonito). It has a delicate and subtle fragrance and flavor |
| Niban dashi | This is a much stronger dashi than the ichiban and is made using the leftover kombu and katsubushi from the ichiban dashi |
| Niboshi dashi | A strong, slightly bitter dashi made using kombu and small dried fish |
| Shojin dashi | This is a vegetarian dashi most commonly made using kombu and shiitake mushrooms |

## The Science of Umami

The savory taste associated with umami is imparted by glutamate, a type of amino acid, and chemicals called ribonucleotides, including inosinate and guanylate, which occur naturally in many foods. There are two forms of glutamate: bound (which form as a part of protein with other amino acids) and free-form (which are found in plant and animal tissues).

Dashi broth with spring onions, sesame and lemon grass makes for a refreshing and flavorsome starter for dinner party guests.

To release the maximum amount of umami most raw foods need to be processed to break down the proteins into free-form amino acids and the nucleic acids into free-form nucleotides. There are various ways to release the umami compounds: boiling, steaming, braising, roasting, salting, smoking, maturing, drying and ageing can all work. However, fermentation is one of the most effective ways to increase umami.

Fermentation involves the use of yeasts and/or bacteria under anaerobic conditions to convert carbohydrates to alcohols and carbon dioxide or organic acids. It is the process used to leaven bread using yeast, and for preservation to produce lactic acid in sour foods including kimchi (a Korean pickled cabbage dish) and yogurt. Fermentation is also responsible for the conversion of sugars into ethanol in the production of alcoholic drinks such as wine and beer. For this reason chefs like René Redzepi (of the restaurant Noma in Denmark) and David Chang (of the momofuku restaurant group in the U.S., Canada and Australia) are dedicating a lot of time to exploring fermentation processes in their research kitchens.

One important point about umami is that when two or more umami-rich ingredients are used together they increase the overall umami taste. This explains classic food pairings such as Parmesan cheese, mushrooms and tomato, chicken and leek soup and even beef burgers with tomato ketchup.

## Umami-rich foods

### SEAFOOD
- Kombu (a type of seaweed)
- Seaweed
- Katsubuoshi (dried, fermented and smoked skipjack tuna)
- Dried bonito flakes (a type of fish)
- Niboshi (small dried sardines)
- Bonito
- Mackerel
- Sea bream
- Tuna
- Cod
- Prawns
- Squid
- Oysters
- Shellfish

### MEAT
- Cured ham
- Duck
- Beef
- Pork
- Chicken

### VEGETABLES
- Tomatoes
- Shiitake mushrooms
- Enokitake mushrooms
- Truffles
- Soy beans
- Potatoes
- Sweet potatoes
- Chinese cabbage
- Carrots

### OTHER
- Parmesan cheese
- Stilton cheese
- Green tea
- Soy sauce
- Oyster sauce
- Chicken eggs
- Walnuts
- Worcestershire sauce
- Human breast milk

# MULTI-SENSORY FLAVOR PERCEPTION

*"Cooking is probably the most multi-sensual art.
I try to stimulate all the senses."*
Ferran Adrià, Head Chef at El Bulli

Food excites our senses, and eating is a multi-sensory
activity as it engages our taste, smell, sight, hearing and
even touch. This chapter looks at how the world's most
acclaimed modern chefs are working with scientists to
engage and heighten their diners' senses, transforming
their meal into an experience.

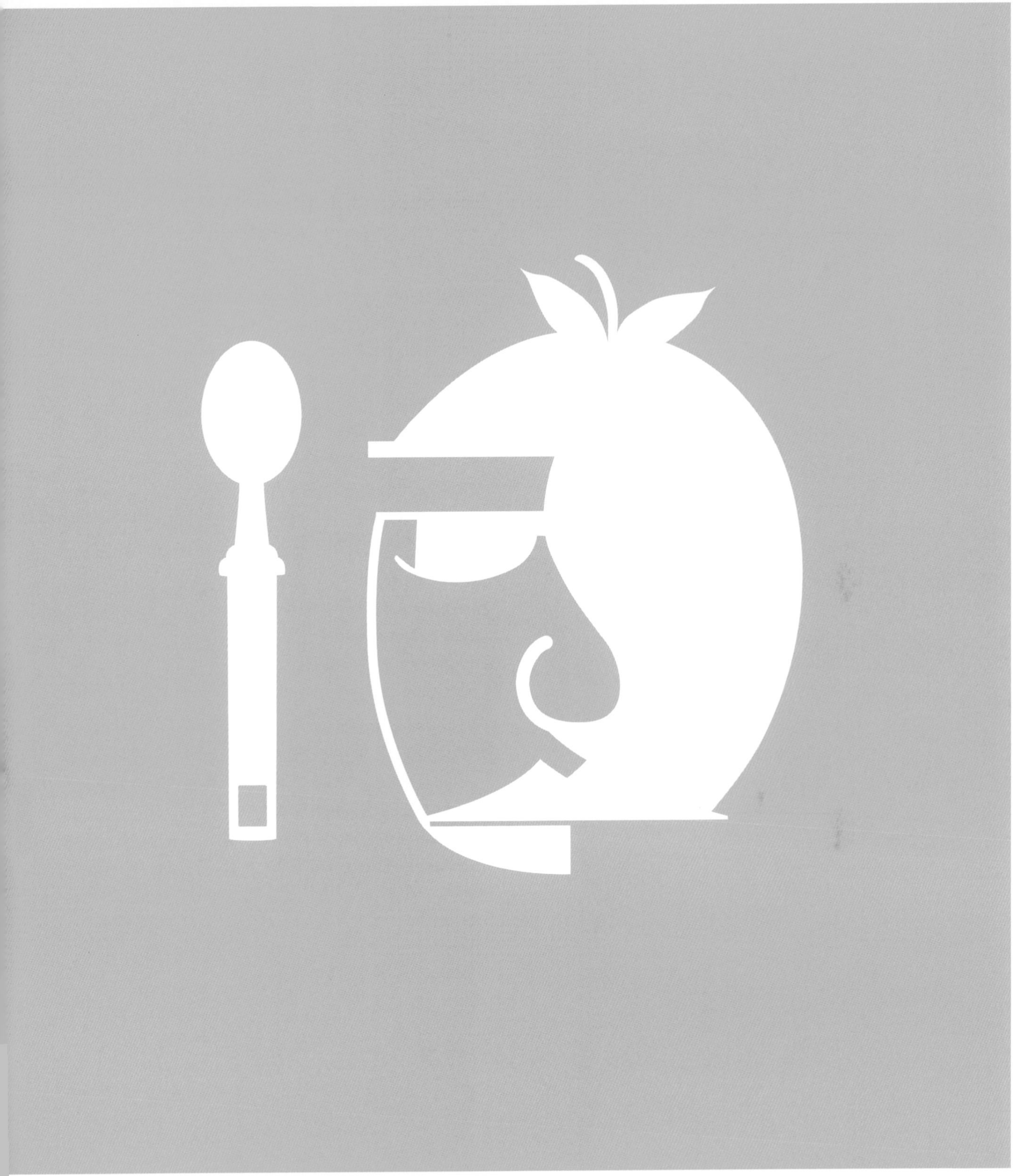

## Our Five Senses

Our five senses are fully engaged while eating. The process begins with our visual and olfactory senses, which see and smell food before we have even begun to consume it. Using these two senses alone we begin to make assumptions and judgments about the food we are about to eat based on the catalog of food-related memories we have stored over time. This means that if your waiter serves you a bowl of lettuce instead of the medium–rare beef you ordered, you will pick up on the cues which make you aware of this mistake without having to actually taste it. Based on the same senses you make decisions about which foods you decide to put on your plate at a buffet and even the foods you decide to buy in the supermarket (packaged products rely more on visual than olfactory cues).

In general the next senses to be engaged are kinesthetic and gustatory, which pick up the cues that inform us about the food's texture and taste. This is how we identify whether the food feels hot or cold, hard or soft, if it is bitter, sweet, sour, salty or high in umami, or perhaps a little of each.

Our auditory sense picks up on the sounds we make during chewing and other oral processing. It lets you know the potato chips are crunchy enough and helps to emphasize other textural sensations. In tests conducted at the Department of Experimental Psychology at Oxford University it was shown that we perceive potato chips as being "fresher" the more crunchy they sound, and that our perception of carbonation in sodas is also dependent on what we hear.

## What is Flavor?

Our five senses work together and none more so than our senses of smell and taste, which combine to allow us to enjoy the flavor of food. Many people confuse the terms "taste" and "flavor." Our sense of taste allows us to pick up on bitterness, sweetness, sourness, saltiness and umami (even pungent, piquant and metallic can be added to this list), while our sense of smell picks up aroma compounds.

Flavor is a complex combination of both senses. To put this idea to the test, eat an orange segment while pinching your nose; you should still be able to taste the sweetness and other related taste sensations, however it will not have a distinct orange flavor. To take your experiment a step further, blindfold a willing test subject and feed them different foods while they pinch their nose and see how accurately they can guess what they are eating. Also note that this is the reason we say we can't "taste" food properly when we have a stuffy nose.

What this experiment should also highlight is that our perception of flavor is heavily influenced by the odors of food. In fact around 80 percent of what makes up our perception of a flavor is based on what we smell, so let's get a better understanding of how our sense of smell works.

When eating there is an initial olfactory stimulation which takes place as our nose picks up aroma substances (volatile compounds), and therefore we smell the aroma of the food before the food is in our mouth — this is called orthonasal detection. Then during the eating process further olfactory stimulation takes place via the throat when, after chewing, the newly released aroma compounds are passed through the back of the mouth to the nose — this is called retronasal detection. Both orthonasal and retronasal detection affect flavor perception.

Aroma is a key part of the multi-sensory experience we achieve with food. Preserve the aroma in a glass food dome for mouth watering results when serving your dish.

### Neurogastronomy

You may be wondering how all this relates to chefs and dining experiences. Well, in recent years chefs have begun working with cognitive psychologists and neuroscientists interested in the topic of multi-sensory taste perception, in the belief that by accentuating or altering certain elements of a dish, whether flavor or presentation, they can enhance a guest's eating experience and engage their senses in unique ways.

Around 40 years ago psychologists and cognitive neuroscientists began studying how our brains process and combine information from what they see, hear and feel. Much research has gone into phenomena such as why it is that people hear better when they put their glasses on, or how we perceive a ventriloquist's dummy as being the one talking even though we know it's not. These forms of multi-sensory research have led to the discovery of a number of fundamental rules which govern multi-sensory perception. These include the fact that vision is our predominant sense, so as with the case of the ventriloquist's dummy, we believe it is the dummy speaking as that is the one whose lips are moving.

In recent years neuroscientists have come to realize that their insights from these studies can be extended to help explain flavor perception, and therefore attention has turned to the ultimate multi-sensory experience of dining. There is much evidence to support the theory that the same fundamental rules apply, and that they can explain why food and drink taste the way they do and why a food may taste good to one person and not so good to another.

In what is now considered a classic experiment, researchers colored a white wine using a red odorless dye and asked a panel of wine experts to describe its taste. The connoisseurs described the wine using typical red wine descriptors rather than terms they would have used to evaluate white wine, suggesting that the color played a significant role in the way they perceived the drink.

Take the ventriloquist example again. As we have already established, we perceive the ventriloquist's dummy as talking because it is the one whose lips are moving so our brain comes to this conclusion because our sense of vision is predominant. A similar phenomenon occurs while we eat. Our sense of taste picks up the five main tastes via the tongue, while much of what creates the flavor of the food lies with the olfactory sense — our nose is capable of picking up and distinguishing up to 10,000 different

research has shown that a strawberry mousse is perceived to be 10 percent sweeter when served on a white plate than on a black one, that serving food on spoons made of different materials affects the way it is perceived, and that even the shape of the plates used to serve food can change our perceptions of a dish.

## Practical Examples

"I say all the time that my mother's Spanish potato and egg tortilla is my favorite, because it conveys a point: that sentimental value comes above all else."

— Ferran Adrià, Head Chef at El Bulli

Other than his research in the lab, Professor Charles Spence has worked with chefs all over the world to develop ideas which have brought new insights to this field of study as well as enhanced the dining experiences at many restaurants. Spence's work with chef Heston Blumenthal of The Fat Duck restaurant in England has resulted in a number of dishes which have now become hallmarks of culinary innovation, including "Egg and Bacon Ice Cream" and "Sounds of the Sea."

The now infamous Egg and Bacon Ice Cream dish started off as tasting nice, but for a restaurant such as The Fat Duck, "nice" just wouldn't cut it — it had to be outstanding. The main issue facing the dish was that the ice cream's two main flavors did not really stand out from one another. Several experiments were conducted until the breakthrough came in the form of the addition of a piece of crispy fried bread. The bread itself did not add much to the dish in

odors. So why is it that we perceive flavor in our mouth rather than our nose? Well, at the time of consuming the food it is in our mouth, where we chew and swallow, and therefore we perceive that all the associated flavors are emanating from the mouth.

One of the leading researchers in the field of neurogastronomy is Professor Charles Spence, head of the Crossmodal Research Laboratory at the Department of Experimental Psychology at Oxford University. He has conducted tests seeking to determine whether it's possible to enhance the taste or flavor of a dish by scientifically matching how, and on what, the food is presented. His

These small vegetable sensory
canapes appeal to every sense.

terms of flavor, however what it managed to do in the eater's mind was "ventriloquize" the bacon; i.e., due to the crispiness of the bread and our associations with "crispy bacon," it seemed to take on the flavor of the bacon while leaving the egg flavor in the more texturally appropriate ice cream.

The Sounds of the Sea consists of several pieces of cured fish served with sea vegetables, edible sand (made using tapioca starch) and a seaweed-based foam. The dish is presented in a manner reminiscent of seabed and sea foam crashing up against a shore. To enhance this seaside experience, guests are presented with an iPod (placed inside a conch shell) which plays a "Sounds of the Sea" track consisting of seagulls squawking, crashing waves and so on. The addition of the soundtrack is not just a gimmicky afterthought; it genuinely engages the guests' auditory

senses which along with the visual cues of the dish and the aquatic flavors all add up to a heightened multi-sensory experience!

The idea behind adding a soundtrack to the Sounds of the Sea dish came as a result of several tests conducted by Blumenthal and Spence, in which they tested people's responses to eating oysters while listening to either "Sounds of the Sea" or a soundtrack of farmyard noises. Participants noted that the oysters tasted significantly better while listening to the "Sounds of the Sea" than when listening to the farmyard noises. Further tests showed that participants could taste the bacon element more distinctly in the Egg and Bacon Ice Cream dish when listening to the sound of sizzling bacon, than when listening to the farmyard soundtrack (which seemed to highlight the ice cream's egg/dairy element).

What these examples show is the importance of all our senses while we eat, and that if you want to create dishes that are exceptionally engaging and memorable it can sometimes require more than just good ingredients and a knowledgeable cook. If you think about it in practical terms, you will find many ways in which our satisfaction with a meal is heavily dependent on multi-sensory elements: how enjoyable would a Michelin star meal be if you had to eat it off a paper plate with plastic cutlery rather than polished silver, or if your table was located next to a noisy construction site rather than a quiet dining room. Does the company you're in make the food taste better? It's most likely that a meal with a loved one in a small café is better than a meal with your worst enemy at the world's best restaurant.

So the next time you are preparing a dinner, take some time to think about how you can add some memorable and engaging elements to your guests' experience.

## Sensory Incongruity

Based on the library of experiences stored in our brain, we have certain expectations and perceptions which we associate with stimuli presented to our senses. The pleasure of food is critically dependent on all sensory attributes being correct, and so food can shock us simply by being served at the wrong temperature, or if it has an inappropriate color. When we order a steak we have certain expectations: that it should feel hot as well as looking, tasting and smelling a particular way. Now if our steak was served and it was a blue color we would immediately have a conflict between our expectations (based on our memories of what a steak should look like) and the blue steak put in front of us. But what would happen when we ate it? Would it still taste the same?

This example of a blue steak (using blue food coloring) is based on an experiment conducted in the 1970s to find out more about the influence of color on our appetite.

Needless to say the participants in the experiment reported feeling rather sick once the lights were turned up and they realized their steak was blue!

What this highlights is sensory incongruity, which is defined as the deliberate mismatching of the sensory attributes of a product (Spence & Piqueras, 2011). The previous example demonstrates a rather negative use of this manipulation. There are, however, some very interesting ways in which this sensory mismatch has been used, an excellent example of which is Chef Heston Blumenthal's "Orange and Beetroot Jelly." Two squares of jelly, one an orange color, the other a deep red, were served on a simple white plate; the guests' flavor expectations were that each of the jellies would match up to the food memory and associations we all have; i.e., that the orange cube would taste of orange and the red cube would taste of beetroot. The guests were then directed to start by trying the orange-colored jelly, only to find that it tasted of beetroot, followed by a further surprise when they tasted the red-colored jelly which tasted of orange! This illusion was created by using blood oranges for the red-colored orange jelly and yellow beetroot for the orange-colored beetroot jelly. This is simplicity at its best, however the profound nature in which this dish engaged the guest and surprised their palate is no small feat.

The lesson here is that a mismatch of senses can stimulate the mind as well as challenge and engage us in new ways, all of which creates a memorable experience. The important point is that this manipulation is done with a lot of thought so that it elicits the right response, as with the Orange and Beetroot Jelly, and avoids turning your guests off their food, as with the blue steak.

# FLAVOR TRIPPING

Here, I am going to talk about synsepalum dulcificum. Before you slam this book shut and get on with cooking some good old wholesome food like your grandmother used to, read on. You are guaranteed to be introduced to an incredibly interesting ingredient that may rock your flavor experience in a way nothing ever has!

Synsepalum dulcificum is more commonly known as the "miracle berry," as well as the "miraculous berry," and resembles a cranberry in appearance. Once consumed, this berry inhibits your ability to perceive sour tastes in food and results in everything tasting sweet! Once you have eaten the fleshy part of the fruit you will be devouring lemons that taste like candy, drinking Guinness that is reminiscent of chocolate milk and cider vinegar that tastes like apple juice!

Although the miracle berry may not be readily available at your local store, you may be able to obtain some through speciality food suppliers. Luckily though, miraculin — the chemical derived from the miracle berry which is responsible for "tricking" your taste buds into sensing sour tastes as sweet — can be bought in the form of pills which are readily available online. It is important to note that miraculin is not a drug and does not affect your mind. It simply alters the way in which your taste buds detect sourness. Your taste buds are affected for anywhere between thirty minutes to one hour, and then you should be back to squirming as you bite into a lemon. Finally, miraculin is legal in the U.S., UK and in most countries around the world.

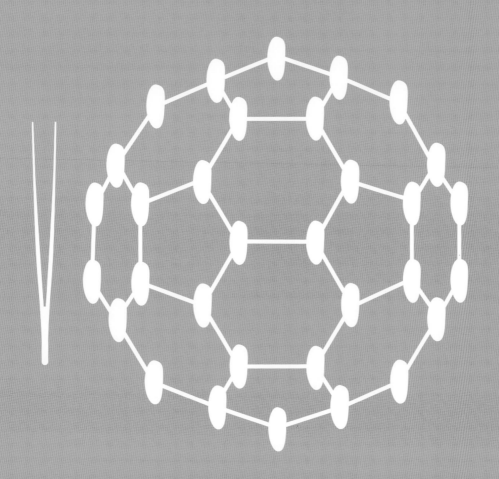

### History

The miracle berry has been consumed for centuries. It originates from tropical West Africa, where it was discovered in 1725 by explorer Chevalier des Marchais during a visit to hunt for new and interesting fruits. Marchais observed the local tribes eating this berry before every meal. Many of their foods were bland and lacking in flavor, so by eating the berry first, the meal was transformed into an enjoyable, flavorsome experience. But it is in the twentieth century that our story with the miracle berry begins.

In the 1960s, Robert Harvey, a biomedical postgraduate student, came across the miracle berry which he believed could hold the key to many health-related issues, including diabetes and obesity. He aimed to develop sweet-tasting foods without sugar or sweeteners, and established the Miralin Company to grow the berry in Jamaica and Puerto Rico, extracting its active ingredient in laboratories in Massachusetts, and marketing it all over the U.S.

Consumer tests showed that foods sweetened by the miracle berry beat those made using sugar in terms of flavor. However, the United States Food and Drug Administration (FDA), which had been supportive of the product and led Harvey to believe that it would be classified as "generally recognized as safe," ruled that it was a food additive that required several years more testing before it would be considered safe for use. There seemed to be no empirical evidence to show that the berry was in any way harmful, and a string of strange events led to the FDA's results. Some people believe that allegations made against the sugar industry led to the sabotage of the project in order to secure the demand for sugar by food manufacturers.

Yet by taking miracle pills, people have been experimenting and "flavor tripping" since the 1970s. The "flavor tripping" phenomenon has now been revived, and "flavor tripping" parties take place all over the world. It has even received attention by modernist chefs, including Homaro Cantu of the Moto restaurant in Chicago, who used the miracle berry in his first cookbook, *The Miracle Berry Diet Cookbook*. In Tokyo The Miracle Fruits Cafe offers desserts that contain 100 calories or less. Their offerings are actually rather bland, with subtle flavors, but once their patrons have eaten the miracle berry the desserts are transformed into enjoyable sweet treats.

### The Science Behind the Miracle Berry and Other Interesting Facts

The miracle berry contains miraculin, a glycoprotein molecule, with some trailing carbohydrate chains. This protein molecule alters your taste receptors by binding to the taste buds and inhibiting sour tastes from being registered. The miraculin induces the sweetness of foods when it comes in contact with acids, causing bitter and sour foods to taste sweet. At neutral pH, miraculin binds and blocks the receptors, but at low pH (resulting from ingestion of sour foods) miraculin binds protons and becomes able to activate the sweet receptors, resulting in the perception of sweet taste. This effect usually lasts between thirty minutes to two hours.

The miracle berry is generally expensive as it rots quickly. A Japanese food importer freeze-dried the berries to preserve them. Even more intriguing, in 2006, a Japanese researcher

The "miracle berry" is similar in appearance to a cranberry.

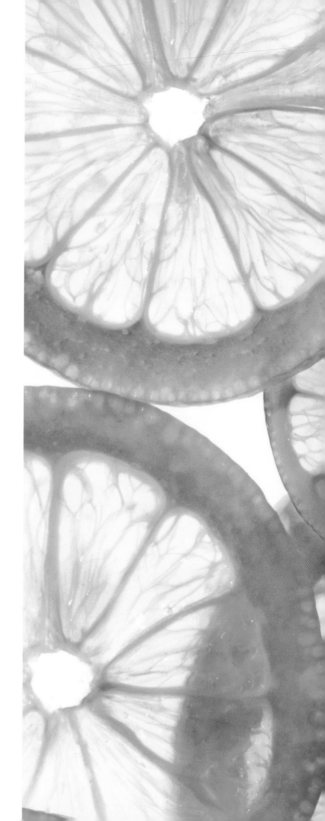

announced that lettuce had been genetically engineered to produce miraculin! If it could be produced in more forms than miracle berries, it may have a wider purpose.

Curculin (found in the fruit of a Malaysian plant) is another protein similar to miraculin. Besides making sour things taste sweet, it also enhances the sweetness of other foods. A main difference is that curculin's effects don't appear to last as long as miraculin's; scientists believe this is due to substances in our saliva which suppress the curculin's effects.

## Flavor Tripping

As mentioned earlier, it is probably easier to get your hands on miraculin pills than the miracle berry itself. Once you have the pills, let them dissolve in your mouth as you roll the pill around on your tongue — don't chew or swallow the pill whole as this will eliminate any of the flavor tripping effects. Once the pill is completely dissolved, you are ready to start tasting! What follows is a list of foods which are definitely worth trying once you have.

- Lemons, grapefruits and limes are fantastic foods to try as their high levels of acidity really bring out the sweetness;

- Fresh fruits such as pineapple, melon and strawberries, as well as blueberries and raspberries, are incredible, their full sweetness and flavor is brought out;

- Carrots and other raw root vegetables can be transformed and have a much sweeter flavor than you would expect.

Citrus fruits take on a new range of flavors when you are flavor tripping with "miracle berries."

# FOOD PAIRING

Traditional food pairing is all about identifying which ingredients go well together, and then using this information to create a dish. There is a plethora of well-known classic food pairings which have been discovered by trial and error and a good dose of intuition, including basil and tomato, apple and pork, cucumber and mint, bacon and cheese, lamb and rosemary, apple and cinnamon, dill and fish, coffee and chocolate . . . and the list goes on.

However, as the modern chef has become more adept at using scientific methods and reasoning in the kitchen, the process of food pairing has taken on a much more scientific approach.

## The Science of Food Pairing

To understand the science of food pairing, we must recap how we perceive flavor (see page 206). We achieve this through two of our senses: taste and smell. From taste we can detect a food's saltiness, sourness, sweetness, bitterness and umami. From smell we detect aroma compounds of which we have the capability of detecting up to 10,000 distinct odors. These two senses do not share an equal contribution to our perception of flavor as around 80 percent of what makes up our perception of a flavor is based on the food's odor.

Scientific food pairing suggests that if two foods have one or more key flavor compounds in common they might go well together and perhaps even complement each other, and that the more compounds foods share the better they should match.

This hypothesis and subsequent trend of pairing flavors based on flavor compounds was first brought to the world's culinary stage by Chef Heston Blumenthal of The Fat Duck restaurant in England. It all began with his experiments with white chocolate. Blumenthal knew that a sprinkle of salt on white chocolate helped to enhance its flavor and temper its sweetness, but he wanted to find out if the effect could be achieved using other "salty" ingredients.

Numerous trials were conducted until he hit upon the unique and complementary combination of white chocolate and caviar. Satisfied with his results, Blumenthal set out to discover why it was that these two foods paired so well. He did this by enlisting the help of François Benzi of Firmenich, the largest privately owned flavor house in the world. Benzi had been researching the concept of food pairing, and at one of the first International Workshops on Molecular Gastronomy had hypothesized that jasmine and pork liver may make a suitable food pairing as they

both contained indole (an aromatic organic compound).

Working together, Blumenthal and Benzi compared white chocolate and caviar and discovered that they shared some major flavor compounds, and the hypothesis was born. Blumenthal then set out to discover further unique food pairings by acquiring the Volatile Compounds in Food database (a commercial database containing information on more than 7,000 volatile molecules in several hundred different foods) and Steffen Arctander's book *Perfume and Flavor Materials of Natural Origin*. Armed with these tools, Blumenthal made a series of unique food pairing discoveries, including caramelized cauliflower and cocoa, strawberry and coriander, mango and violet, chocolate and pink peppercorn, chocolate and smoked eel, salmon and licorice and oysters and passion fruit.

So based on this hypothesis there are numerous potential food combinations out there based solely on their flavor compounds. This is in many ways revolutionary in the culinary world, as it lifts all the restrictions and influence of tradition, culture and old-school ways of thinking, opening the door to a whole host of new and interesting food combinations. So far this unrestricted way of thinking has led to chefs all around the world producing new dishes with unique flavors.

It is also important to note that this hypothesis has proven to hold up when put to the test with traditional food pairings like those mentioned earlier in the chapter, so basil and tomatoes do in fact share flavor compounds, as do bacon and cheese.

One further interesting point to mention is that a 2011 Harvard University study by Yong-Yeol Ahn, in which he analyzed the network of links between the ingredients and flavors in 56,000 recipes, concluded that the food pairing hypothesis holds in Western Europe and North America, but in Southern Europe and East Asia a converse principle of anti-pairing seems to be at work!

## Food Pairing Methodology

You may be wondering how foods are analyzed for the purpose of food pairing. Firstly, a food's aroma compounds are identified using gas chromatography and measured using a mass spectrometer. From this analysis the food's key odorants are determined. Many foods have several thousand aroma compounds, many of which humans cannot detect (they are considered lower than our flavor threshold); key odorants on the other hand are the compounds that we are able to smell. These key odorants compose the flavor profile of the food, and this profile is then compared to several hundred other foods in a database. The result is that foods that share common key odorants are highlighted, and it is then up to the chefs to go away and find innovative ways of bringing these ingredients together in one spectacular dish.

By now you must be wondering how on Earth you are going to use food pairing as a tool to improve your own cooking, especially given your lack of chemistry lab equipment and access to commercial flavor compound databases. Rest assured that the bulk of the hard work is being taken care of for you and that there are a growing number of websites offering free and subscription-based services which allow you to log on and have access to a growing database of established food pairings; simply search for "food pairing" on the Internet and let the fun begin.

Salmon with licorice is an innovative flavor combination.

# FOOD PRESENTATION

On pages 206–213, we looked at the importance of multi-sensory flavor perception — how our five senses affect the way in which we perceive flavor — and highlighted the fact that our sense of sight is our dominant sense. Even when eating our sense of sight is of the highest importance as we use it to make all sorts of judgments about a food before we even lift our knife and fork. Many cultures say "you eat with your eyes first"; this idea has only become popular in Western kitchens for the past few decades, however in some parts of the world, especially Japan, this philosophy is one of the cuisine's foundations.

As with any art form, cooking allows for a great deal of self-expression. The world's top chefs all tend to have a signature style which can range from earthy, organic and rustic, to modern, minimal and scientific. These signature styles are honed over the length of a chef's career, and as any top chef will tell you, their style is constantly evolving and developing to incorporate new influences. It can be influenced by other chefs, by new cooking methods, by traveling to new destinations and learning about other cultures, even by other forms of art; as far back as the 18th century, some of the great Marie-Antoine Carême's *pièces montées* (large, decorative centerpieces) were influenced by architectural monuments.

So allow yourself to express your own individuality through your cooking and develop your signature style based on what you are passionate about. But remember, as with any art it is important that you master the basics first, as only once you have this solid foundation can you competently begin to build up your own creative style.

## The Art and Philosophy of Japanese Food Presentation

It would be impossible to overlook Japanese cuisine in a chapter on food presentation. Not only have the Japanese refined this aspect of cooking, they have inspired the rest of the world with their emphasis on the importance of the balance between seasonality (the consumption of ingredients while at their best) and the visual simplicity, harmony and elegance with which they present their dishes.

For the Japanese chef, food presentation is a philosophical matter, much of which is dependent on the current season and the occasion for which they are cooking. Japan has very distinct seasons both in terms of the weather and of course the ingredients available, each season providing chefs with a different palate of ingredients to work with. It is equally important to the Japanese chef that their dishes should echo the seasonality of the food through the use of different chinaware, so lighter colored flower-patterned crockery in spring and darker leaf-patterned crockery in fall. There are seven plating methods in Japanese cuisine:

1. Sugimori is a standing or slanting arrangement.

2. Hiramori is a flat design with slices of sashimi placed vertically.

3. Yamamori is mound-like.

4. Tawaramori are blocks of food placed in a pyramid.

5. Yosemori is gathered.

6. Chirashimori is gathered, but with space between the ingredients.

7. Ayamori is woven.

The use of color is equally important in reflecting the season on the plate. Colors relating to seasons include white for winter, pink and green for spring, red and green or purple for summer, orange and yellow for fall. Red and gold can be used for special occasions, while silver and black relate to mourning.

Japanese cuisine has dramatically influenced Western cuisine in more ways than one. In 1960 Shizuo Tsuji opened the first French culinary school in Japan, resulting in a greater culinary cultural exchange between the Japanese and leading French chefs. At the same time there was a growing interest in Japanese cuisine by some of France's most influential chefs, including the legendary Paul Bocuse. Until this point French cuisine was rather rich and heavy and lacked any real visual appeal. French plating focused on showing all the ingredients side by side, or they would also be stacked by placing the main ingredient on a bed of vegetables. So in their quest to refine French cuisine into what we now term "nouvelle cuisine," these French chefs became attracted to unusual and exotic foods, and Japanese cuisine successfully captured their imaginations. There are certain elements of nouvelle cuisine which have been heavily inspired by Japanese cuisine, especially the emphasis on food presentation, seasonality on the plate and simplicity. Another interesting note is that Kaiseki — a traditional Japanese meal which consists of multiple small courses — was a direct influence behind the multi-course tasting menus available in most of the world's top restaurants today.

Greens , oranges and yellows denote a dish full of fall flavors. The relating of colors to seasons is typical of Japanese food presentation.

## Food Presentation Notes

Some chefs like to use large white plates to "frame" or "showcase" their food. The important point here is to make sure your portions are suitable for the size of the plate you are using. Just as it can be unappetizing to have a whole mountain of food piled on your plate, it can be equally off-putting and take away from the dish's impact if there is just not enough food on the plate.

Smaller portions are generally more interesting to play with and can be more elegant and visually appealing on the plate. But don't get this concept confused with a typical 1980s nouvelle cuisine stereotype of a carrot and pea lost on a large white plate. If you decide to opt for smaller portions, you should add more ingredients and detail to the dish; this might also mean you serve four smaller courses instead of three regular-sized portions.

Make sure the different food elements of your dish are proportionally balanced. You don't want to overload your dish with a foam, purée or sauce, for example. Make sure it is proportional to the other elements of the dish. Also consider how to get the best impact from each ingredient. The appearance and symmetry of a dish is affected by whether an ingredient is sliced thin, thick or left whole.

Focus on vibrant colors. When designing each dish make sure that your ingredients not only pair well together but add different colors and textures; some may complement one another, others may contrast, all of which is important toward building a balanced dish.

The symmetrical application of sauce and the carefully placed central ingredients create a pleasing arrangement in this dish.

Different presentation methods give a different feel, even when the same ingredients are used. Stacking (see above) creates a hearty and wholesome vibe, while a scattering effect (see left) gives the impression that every mouthful should be savored.

Use seasonal ingredients — they will taste and look better as they are at their best.

Elevation. Not to be confused with piling all your food into ridiculous towers, a method of presentation that has become over-used, dated and heavily mocked. The idea of adding height to your dish is still important as it gives the dish an added dimension. Herbs and garnishes such as Parmesan or bacon crisps are ideal for a bit of upward volume.

For some dishes it may be a good idea to use plating molds in which you can place the food so that when you remove it the shape is maintained. Plating molds are extremely useful tools for professional chefs who wish to create more modern-looking dishes. The point to keep in mind is not to overdo it: use molds when plating but try to make the overall result appear natural, organic and free-flowing. Geometric-shaped food is not really that appetizing and too much of it on one plate will take away from how good your food actually tastes.

Repetition in odd numbers seems to be a key design rule in areas other than food, but it does actually look better. So if you are putting identical pieces of food on the plate, use either three or five pieces. For example, if you are creating a ravioli pasta starter, use three small pieces; if it is a main course use five larger pieces.

Make sure you are cooking the right food for the right occasion. Pie and mashed potato may taste great, but it's near impossible to make a dish like this look good enough for a refined dinner party while maintaining the dish's essential characteristics.

Remember that as with stacking food in towers, all food presentation trends eventually become outdated, so keep ahead of the curve by watching cooking shows, reading food magazines and most importantly going online and

visiting the websites of top restaurants and chefs to see what they are doing.

The Japanese use mismatched crockery for each course, unlike in the West where the tendency is to use one matching set of crockery. This is an interesting concept as it allows you to match different plates or bowls with each course you are serving. Perhaps your salad starter looks better on a white plate, but the vanilla ice cream dessert looks better in a black bowl. There is an abundance of interesting crockery available: look in Asian and Middle Eastern stores, craft or flea markets and antique stores. Other novel ideas include hollowing out large bread rolls to use as soup bowls, while coconut shells, banana leaves or scallop shells can make for an interesting service piece. So use your crockery as part of the dish's overall appeal, and don't be afraid to mix and match as long as it makes sense and does your food justice.

Finally, it is of the upmost importance that you keep to the following fundamental principle at all times: *presentation should not compromise the taste, temperature or practicality of your dish.*

Use non-edible garnishes such as flowers to "prop" your plate and bring out the colorful flavors.

## Co
**Core temperature**

The temperature at the "core" of a food. It is important that meat reaches a particular internal temperature before becoming safe to consume.

# GLOSSARY

## Cu
**Culinary foam**

A liquid (such as juice, purée or soup) mixed with a gelling or stabilizing agent and aerated with a hand-held immersion blender.

## De
**Dehydration**

Dehydration is a the technique in which foods are dried out at relatively low temperatures; typically around 176°F (80°C) or lower.

## Di
**Digital probe thermometer**

These are digital thermometers with a probe attached which allows you to take accurate core/internal food termperature readings.

## Es
**Espuma**

Also called a "siphon" or a "whipper" these are basically the professional chef's equivalent of a reusable whipped cream canister.

## Fl
**Flavor**

Flavor is a complex combination of our senses of taste and smell.

## Ga
**Gas chargers**

iSi whippers can be used with both N2O and CO2 gas cartridges to make airy concoctions or fizzy ones respectively.

## Ge
**Gel**

By weight gels are mostly liquid, however, they behave like a solid material. They have a jelly-like consistency and texture.

## Ha
**Hand held immersion blender**

Also called a stick blender, these are becoming a more and more common appliance found in home kitchens.

## Hy
**Hydrocolloid**

In very simple terms a hydrocolloid can be defined as a substance that forms a gel in contact with water to thicken, gel and stabilize.

## Im
**Immersion circulator**

Circulates and heats a warm fluid at an accurate and stable temperature, but more sophisticated than a water-bath.

## Mi
**Millard reaction**

"Caramelization'"or "browning," the dark brown color that food takes on when grilled or fried occurs when proteins in meat heat to around 310°F (154°C).

| Mono-sodium glutamate |
| :---: |
| # Mo |
| Also known as MSG, it is the sodium salt of glutamic acid, one of the most abundant naturally occurring non-essential amino acids. |

| Multi sensory flavor perception | Polyscience | Sol | Sous-vide | Spherification |
| :---: | :---: | :---: | :---: | :---: |
| **Mu** | **Po** | **So** | **So** | **Sp** |
| An area of study focused on how we percieve, taste and interact with food. | An American company which has developed highly innovative kitchen appliances for forward thinking and scientifically minded chefs. | A sol is a colloidal suspension of very small solid particles in a continuous liquid medium; examples are milk, ink or blood. | A French term which literally translates to "under vacuum." As a cooking term it refers to poaching food vacuum sealed in a plastic bag. | A culinary process in which flavored liquids are manipulated to form a thin membrane around the liquid and form spherical capsules. |

| Taste | Transglutaminase | Water-bath |
| :---: | :---: | :---: |
| **Ta** | **Tr** | **Wa** |
| Our sense of taste allows us to pick up on bitterness, sweetness, sourness, saltiness and umami (even pungent or piquant). | Transglutaminase is a naturally occurring enzyme with the ability to bond animal tissue. Its less technical name amongst chefs is "meat glue." | A temperature controlled water basin typically used to cook foods which have been vaccum packed. |

# INDEX

Page numbers in *italic* refer to illustrations

REFERENCES

Blumenthal, H. (2008). *The Big Fat Duck Cookbook*. London: Bloomsbury.

Brillat-Savarin, J.A. (1825). *Physiologie du Goût [The Philosopher in the Kitchen / The Physiology of Taste]*. J.P. Meline: Bruxelles. Translated by A. Lalauze (1884), *A Handbook of Gastronomy*. London: Nimmo & Bain.

McGee, H. (1990). *The Curious Cook*. New York: Collier Books.

Shepherd, G.M. (2012). *Neurogastronomy: How the Brain Creates Flavor and Why it Matters*. New York: Columbia University Press.

Spence, C., & Piqueras-Fiszman, B. (in press). *The Perfect Meal*. Oxford: Wiley.

DISCLAIMER

All practices suggested in this book are considered safe for home use. However neither the author nor publisher accept liability for any of the recipes or techniques. If in doubt, contact your ingredient or equipment supplier.